THE SURVIVE AND THRIVE TOOLKIT FOR LEADERS

Praise for
The Survive and Thrive Toolkit for Leaders

"Monique is a force to be listened to for anyone looking to become a business leader. As a person who has gone through so much and has so much empathy, she brings a refreshing view of leadership that is often lacking in the business world. Her book draws from both personal traumas and victories to explore how each of us has potential to rise above our past and become the best version of ourselves."

—**RYAN TANAKA**, startup sales veteran and personal running coach

"Although geared toward corporate leaders, *The Survive and Thrive Toolkit for Leaders* is truly a guide for leaders in any space looking to improve themselves and their work environment. Daigneault provides no-nonsense, succinct, and actionable guidance in this thorough toolkit that is certain to bring results to leaders ready to work for change."

—**HEATHER ZYGMONTOWICZ**, City of Detroit government program director

"Monique Daigneault, as an accomplished executive coach, provides a clearly illuminated path to achieve greater organizational impact by focusing first on your own well-being. A great read that causes reflection and creates action."

—**RICHARD WEYLMAN**, two-time international bestselling author, hall of fame professional speaker, and Customer Experience Hall of Fame inductee

THE SURVIVE AND THRIVE TOOLKIT FOR LEADERS

How to Lead with Intention
to Transform Your Business
and Exceed Your Goals

by
MONIQUE DAIGNEAULT

CORAL GABLES

Copyright © 2024 by Monique Daigneault.
Published by Mango Publishing, a division of Mango Publishing Group, Inc.

Cover Illustration: MD Consulting

Mango is an active supporter of authors' rights to free speech and artistic expression in their books. The purpose of copyright is to encourage authors to produce exceptional works that enrich our culture and our open society.

Uploading or distributing photos, scans or any content from this book without prior permission is theft of the author's intellectual property. Please honor the author's work as you would your own. Thank you in advance for respecting our author's rights.

For permission requests, please contact the publisher at:
Mango Publishing Group
2850 S Douglas Road, 2nd Floor
Coral Gables, FL 33134 USA
info@mango.bz

For special orders, quantity sales, course adoptions and corporate sales, please email the publisher at sales@mango.bz. For trade and wholesale sales, please contact Ingram Publisher Services at customer.service@ingramcontent.com or +1.800.509.4887.

The Survive and Thrive Toolkit for Leaders: How to Lead with Intention to Transform Your Business and Exceed Your Goals

Library of Congress Cataloging-in-Publication number: 2024938221
ISBN: (p) 978-1-68481-625-5, (e) 978-1-68481-626-2
BISAC category code BUS046000, BUSINESS & ECONOMICS / Motivational

TABLE OF CONTENTS

Introduction	9

PILLAR ONE

Introduction	19
Chapter 1: Physical Wellness	21
Chapter 2: Intellectual Wellness	44
Chapter 3: Emotional Wellness	54
Chapter 4: Relationship Wellness	65
Chapter 5: Spiritual Wellness	78
Chapter 6: Environmental Wellness	92
Chapter 7: Occupational Wellness	104
Chapter 8: Financial Wellness	116

PILLAR TWO

Introduction	129
Chapter 9: Being Aligned with Your Values	133
Chapter 10: Influencing Organizational Behavior and Company Culture	142
Chapter 11: Implementing Company-Wide Change	151
Chapter 12: Leveraging Your Strengths to Navigate Roadblocks	166
Chapter 13: Comprehending and Communicating Your Vision, Mission, and Goals	177
Chapter 14 : Communicating Effectively to Solve Business Problems	189
Chapter 15: Building Strong Business Relationships through Networking	207
Chapter 16: Tying It All Together	221

Concluding Thoughts	224
Bibliography	226
References	229
Index	233
About the Author	240

INTRODUCTION

My Trauma and Corporate Experience

We all have a story to tell, and mine is one of surviving multiple childhood traumas. After escaping my home situation and first marriage, I could have easily ended up a drug dealer, an addict, homeless, in prison, or worse. I am still not sure how those things did not happen. I believe I used my anger and fear to fuel my survival. One trauma after another taught me new skills, increased my agility, and built my resilience. I unknowingly tapped into my intuition, internal fortitude, and self-discipline—allowing these principles to guide my actions. On some level, I realized that growing up in an abyss of violence and shame did not have to define me, it would not define my children, and I did not have to continue the cycle.

As a single parent of two daughters, I entered the corporate world with a bit of an attitude at age twenty-two. I had no college degree, but had earned my GED after getting married and dropping out of high school. I assumed that working in a business environment was the best way to make a living, since I was not receiving child support. Unfortunately, what I saw there was more suffering. Fear, intimidation, bias, discrimination, incivility, and disrespect were rampant. I soon realized that my style at work (and in life) was to rock the boat, advocate for others, and disrupt the status quo when necessary. I am an introvert by nature, and luckily for me, I learned that change happens more quickly with actions than with words. Since then, feedback from others has validated that my demeanor is one of quiet strength and courage that makes a big impact and influences others. I now leverage that!

I realized that my quiet strength gave me the gift of facilitating transformation. Since most business problems are caused by human behavior, I decided to focus my mission on shifting behavior in the workplace. Once a high school dropout, I have now combined my hands-on business experience with formal education. I have completed two business degrees, a master's of science degree in organizational psychology, and seven additional certifications. Plus, I have developed a unique skill of harnessing the transformative power of trauma by leveraging my condition of complex post-traumatic stress disorder (cPTSD).

Many people have experienced either full-blown trauma or various microtraumas, but instead of embracing powerful lessons, they have remained stuck there. I have found my way out, although my healing is a continuous journey. While I cannot change my past, I can certainly use that experience to shape workplace culture and to guide others toward transformation. Whether you are a corporate leader in the workplace who has experienced past trauma, a corporate leader who is currently experiencing trauma in the workplace, or a corporate leader who wants to learn how to proactively lead through dysfunction, my tools will become your tools.

MICROTRAUMA IN THE WORKPLACE

Isn't it ironic that, even though corporations exist to solve customers' problems, they also are the source of many employees' problems? It would be nice and comforting if I could paint a rosy picture of the typical workplace environment. But that is not what I have experienced, nor is it what my clients see on a daily basis. I have been a trained executive coach since 2003, working with executives worldwide in over twenty industries. During decades of coaching corporate leaders, I have helped those who struggle with impostor syndrome, decision-making, low self-confidence, presentation anxiety, transitioning to new roles, professional branding, job searching, giving and receiving feedback, conducting difficult conversations, starting a business, leading teams, handling conflict, and many other complex workplace situations. I have witnessed leaders who struggle with microtraumas in the workplace, those grappling with their own past trauma, and those trying to help their teams navigate in a trauma-filled environment. When these things come up in coaching, I have woven my processes, tools, and systems into the coaching relationship with great success for the client.

In addition to full-blown workplace violence, employees are also dealing with a more subtle form of trauma in the very place where they spend most of their life. Microtraumas occur daily in the workplace, but because the events are seemingly insignificant, they tend to be ignored and are therefore allowed to continue. Over time, this steady stream of events can build up, causing psychological harm to the self-worth, security, and productivity of an individual or team. Some examples of workplace microtraumas are a controlling or egotistical boss, insults, gaslighting, withholding praise or feedback, withholding pay, bonuses, or promotions, or having unrealistic and unclear expectations, minimizing one's concerns, overt or covert threats, coercion, passive-aggressive behavior, anger, indifference, shaming, manipulation, and bullying.

This behavior is contradictory to the critical psychological safety that is much needed in the workplace. Psychological safety is the belief that employees can speak up, ask questions, make mistakes, and take risks without fear of punishment, humiliation, or retaliation. Employees who feel psychologically safe are more likely to be creative, innovative, collaborative, and happy in their jobs. Microtraumatic environments leave a person or a team feeling fearful, helpless, shamed, vulnerable, and held hostage. Yes, held hostage. I say this because it is rare that someone can even recognize a microtrauma for what it is in the moment. And, if they do, can they navigate those circumstances with enough skill and experience to address it? Sometimes the only option to break the cycle is for the person to quit their job. However, many people cannot do that, for a variety of reasons. I can only speak for myself as a former single parent and from what I hear from the clients I coach daily, but it is highly uncommon that a person can simply quit their job without having a second one lined up. They are accustomed to a certain salary, benefit package, work schedule, retirement plan, professional network, and lifestyle. So, yes, in a sense they are held hostage and become caught up in a daily barrage of second-guessing themselves, confusion, anxiety, and fear. The impact of microtraumas reduces work-life balance and productivity. On top of that, they increase stress, health issues, absenteeism, and attrition.

Repeated exposure to workplace microtraumas is a form of traumatic stress and has similar symptoms to post-traumatic stress disorder (PTSD). According to many published studies about PTSD, the symptoms are generally grouped into four types: intrusive memories, avoidance, negative changes in thinking and mood, and changes in physical and emotional reactions. Symptoms can vary over time and differ from person to person.

Although many of my clients routinely experience these symptoms from microtraumas, let me use a personal example to illustrate how an experience of bullying caused these symptoms for me. In a previous corporate position, my manager routinely and subtly put me down in front of my teammates, used a condescending tone, and covertly threatened my job standing in private. The only feedback I received from her was negative, and when I asked for direction so I that could improve, she provided ambiguous responses. When I then asked for clarity around the ambiguousness, she became annoyed and said I asked too many questions. Yet, when I tried to improve without her mentoring, I was reprimanded for not being on the same page. It was only when I reported her behavior to Human Resources that she finally backed down.

During this time, which lasted about one year, I had nightmares (intrusive memories), became afraid to schedule meetings with my boss (avoidance), developed negativity and depression (mood changes), and had high anxiety, irritability, and trouble sleeping (changes in physical and emotional reactions). Normally a highly productive person, my productivity dropped considerably, based on peer feedback, during that time. As a survivor of complex childhood trauma, I am already extremely sensitive to dysfunctional behavior. As you will learn throughout this book, this episode of bullying was unfortunately only one of many microtraumas I experienced during my corporate career.

THE BROKEN LEADER

As if dysfunctional workplace behavior is not already devastating enough, the deeper issue is that it ruins profoundly good leaders. Employees at all levels have the spirit whipped out of them and are left feeling broken, subjugated, defeated, incompetent, and somehow "less than." These are people who absolutely love their jobs and are trying to make a company-wide difference through their management of their own teams. They are trying to develop teams, help customers, contribute to their organization's mission, mentor and coach coworkers, and be a part of something bigger.

Away from the office, they are also trying to support families and set a good example on a personal level. They are trying to lead at home, in the community, and in the workplace. They are good leaders trying to be better leaders.

But they get caught in the abyss of dysfunction and they do not know how to escape. While it is true that many people leave one organization and go to another, they will likely find the same problem with the new company. It happened to me, and it is happening to my clients.

WHO IS THIS BOOK FOR?

While this book may speak to anyone in the workforce, it is specifically intended for corporate middle and senior management executives who are experiencing dysfunctional workplace culture. They are those I refer to as "trauma-sensitive" leaders. These leaders are ambitious, career-driven, educated individuals who are trying to make a difference in the workplace. Yet they are repeatedly subjected to behavior from their peers and other senior leaders that is condescending, inconsistent, and degrading.

Many have also experienced trauma outside of work that they have never addressed, which makes them extremely sensitive to workplace trauma. Even if they have not experienced personal or workplace trauma, they are aware of direct reports who have, and they do not have the tools to help either themselves or others. Some, like me, also have the Highly Sensitive Person (HSP) character trait, making them more sensitive to trauma than their non-HSP counterparts. The HSP trait is a highly misunderstood, innate characteristic found in 15-20 percent of the population and is characterized by a high sensitivity to environments. This was my situation. I experienced complex childhood trauma as well as workplace trauma, and I carry the HSP trait. The people I coach daily are, at the very least, experiencing traumatic work environments, and they are the reason I know that this problem persists. I naively thought that the dysfunctional workplace had gotten better since I retired from the corporate world. Unfortunately, that is not the case.

In order to combat these lingering issues, I have structured my coaching methodology around a process to help individuals not only survive, but also thrive, by leveraging the transformational power of trauma. This book is for three types of leaders who may or may not be HSPs: good leaders who want to transform themselves into better leaders, leaders who have had past trauma and are now in the workplace possibly being triggered by more trauma, and leaders who are experiencing workplace trauma for the first time.

While you can close a skills gap with more education, staying one hundred percent relevant in any job role with any company requires more. You need to know how to transform yourself and then use that influence to transform your organization and your team. Once you harness the strategies from this book, you will no longer feel frustrated, broken, and demeaned, and wonder if the effort you put into your career has been worthwhile. You will no longer question whether you are making a difference. You will actively handle workplace microtraumas and dysfunctional behavior with grace, empowerment, and confidence. I can tell you for a fact that my clients who are doing this are out to make a difference and they are succeeding. What is the answer to shifting workplace dysfunction? You are the answer! And you will learn how by reading this book.

HOW YOU WILL BENEFIT FROM THIS BOOK

This book will help you recognize personal, professional, and leadership gaps that may be holding you back. You will also pinpoint areas where you might be sabotaging yourself and succumbing to your own victimhood. You will be using tools and techniques that I learned in my trauma work to overcome your stuck points. The most important thing I have learned on my journey is to immediately apply new skills and knowledge. For many, this is a new process, and you will be flexing a new muscle. I will be sharing my journey with you along the way, so that, hopefully, you will not feel alone.

While completing these exercises, you will then learn how to influence your organization in a more impactful way. Your confidence level will be increasing every day due to your personal work, so practicing your new skills in real-time work situations is the ideal training ground. At the organizational and strategic level, you will be influencing culture and addressing any microtrauma you may be witnessing or experiencing. All the while, you will be exerting a more powerful leadership presence.

Your growth will impact your team. They deserve to be developed, mentored, and coached in a healthy way so that they do not have the same negative workplace experiences you encountered. They are our future corporate leaders, and you have a responsibility to them. I will address many common challenges of running a team and how you can handle them with your newfound skills. Throughout the book, you will be building resilience and self-discipline, increasing cognitive agility, and learning to trust your intuition to better lead with quiet strength and influence.

HOW TO USE THIS BOOK

Throughout the book, you will have the benefit of reading about my own experiences and those of actual clients. The names and certain details of personal stories will be altered to protect anonymity and privacy.

The book is divided into two pillars that follow my coaching model of transforming yourself and transforming your organization. It is best to begin from the start of the first pillar and read it through to the end of the second pillar, because your personal transformation (Pillar One) will impact your ability to transform the organization (Pillar Two). Throughout each chapter, you will be prompted to reflect, journal, and complete actions so that you can apply what you've learned as you go. If you need additional support, you can register for individual coaching with me and the online training program that is based on this book. The structure of the book allows you to reread and focus on sections that you find most applicable to your own career and transformation. Reading this book is a relatively short commitment, but the techniques you will develop within each of the chapters result in a lifelong payoff. If you can shift your mindset in these areas, you can powerfully impact the workplace. You owe this to yourself.

PILLAR ONE

TRANSFORM YOURSELF BY INTEGRATING EIGHT DIMENSIONS

Pillar One

INTRODUCTION

Most of the leaders I coach are burned-out, feel overwhelmed, and have an insufficient work-life balance. Due to the challenges of their jobs, they have developed poor nutrition, exercise, and mental health habits. Their social lives are subpar, they have had to give up hobbies they once enjoyed, their home life is suffering, and they show up for work exhausted. This impacts how they perform at work, and how they influence their team. When I entered the corporate world at age twenty-two, the odds were against me. At the time, I was undiagnosed with cPTSD, a single parent with two young children, an HSP, an introvert, and going through a divorce. As I became more embedded in my job, I was subjected to widespread dysfunction in the workplace. That is when my healing journey began, and it has never stopped. For a long time, I kept hoping for the moment when the journey would be complete, when I could shout from the rooftops that I had finally healed, that I had "arrived." But over time, I realized the important truth that healing, growth, and transformation are never over. They are continuous acts of courage.

An important point that I want to stress here is that your journey as a person, a leader, or a trauma survivor is ongoing. And if you happen to be a leader who is also a trauma survivor, or a leader dealing with current trauma, then your journey may be more difficult. This is especially so if you are also an HSP. It will never be over, but that is not a bad thing. As a matter of fact, consider yourself blessed, because you can more powerfully transform yourself and others.

I am going to give you the tools that you need to reshape your relationship with your profession, your coworkers, and your workplace, and I urge you to make the most of them. I have an extraordinarily strong intuition and an ability to adapt and survive most situations. At age twenty-two, as I began to blaze the trail of my own survival, I was healing multiple dimensions of my life simultaneously. I did not realize until many years later that I had been intuitively strengthening the Eight Dimensions of Wellness. The Dimensions of Wellness model was originally created by Dr. Bill Hettler, co-founder of the National Wellness Institute, in 1976. He originally created a six-dimension model to teach the public how all areas of our life are interconnected and create a holistic sense of wellness and fulfillment. Since then, the model has evolved and shifted to include seven and even eight dimensions. The next eight chapters will orient you to the concept of the Eight Dimensions of Wellness that I used in my healing journey.

As you work through this pillar, you will be creating your version of wellness in all eight areas, prioritizing your goals, identifying deep behaviors that are keeping you stuck, and implementing long-lasting solutions. Remember that transformation is nonlinear, and you must be patient with yourself. Completing the work in this pillar will give you a solid foundation and prepare you for the tougher work within your organization. It will also have you feeling stronger and more confident in your own skin so that you can take on Pillar Two.

Chapter 1

PHYSICAL WELLNESS

Are you working so many hours that you don't have balance in your life? Do you really think you are accomplishing what you need to during all those extra hours? Think again! Successful leaders operate from a place of peak performance. By conditioning your mind and body and working at your peak performance, you are modeling behaviors that will help your team. You are setting a good example and influencing them to also strive for balance. Here is what a peak-performing team looks like:

- Low absenteeism = high motivation
- Low stress = high productivity and efficiency
- More rest and relaxation = better collaboration and more impactful decisions

Do you want to be in better mental and physical health and influence your team to adopt the same mindset? If so, there are some important things you need to know about physical wellness and peak performance. We will delve into strategies like how to increase your daily energy with exercise and nutrition, how to clear your head during the day with certain mental techniques, and how to stay centered during tough negotiations.

Improving your physical wellness will help you become fit for leadership. This dimension focuses on caring for your body by increasing endurance, strength, and flexibility through structured exercise. You will also learn about the importance of nutrition, supplementation, and basic self-care.

Exercise has been my lifeline for decades. During my childhood trauma experiences, I learned to disconnect from my bodily sensations and emotions. This learned behavior served me well as a survival mechanism while growing up. But as an adult, I was unable to stay present, self-regulate, and manage my emotions when faced with stress or various types of microtraumas. By my early twenties, I was experiencing chest pains, anxiety attacks, chronic coughing, yellowed fingernails, illnesses, insomnia, and chronic fatigue. That was my wake-up call. During my first divorce, I suddenly began to think about my health and was intuitively drawn toward exercise. I initially began riding an exercise bike, and suddenly my insomnia improved. While I was in my marriage, exercise was not part of my life because I was constantly in survival mode. Then, I finally made the connection between body and mind—body and stress level. It felt like I had discovered gold!

Currently, I have a very robust daily embodiment practice. An embodiment practice is a method of using the unique sensations of our body as a tool to develop awareness, stay present, self-regulate, feel whole, find balance, feel connected, know ourselves, love ourselves, and be empowered. Exercise did that for me, well before I knew what an embodiment practice was, and it can help you too.

Many of my clients do not have a consistent exercise routine due to time constraints, a heavy workload, and personal commitments. At first, exercise was not consistent for me either.

Your physical wellness is *your* responsibility, and you must get engaged in the process. If you are a parent, your number-one focus is your child's health, yet how often do we give that importance to our own well-being? And think about how much better your parenting can be if your health is in order. Start slow, by paying attention to everything that goes into your body and how you feel afterwards. Be aware of your activity level, your sleep patterns, and your moods. Be your own advocate. You have complete control over your physical wellness—it is a matter of using the three-P methodology:

- Priorities
- Progress
- Patience

Prioritize your life so that your physical wellness is high on the list.

Progress only happens when you have consistency. So that means committing to a well-balanced lifestyle.

Patience is the only way you will keep your sanity when altering a lifetime of poor health habits.

One tool to use when making huge life changes is a journal. I will refer to this tool constantly throughout this book. For this chapter, I will refer to it as an exercise journal, but in later chapters, I will recommend journaling in other ways and for various reasons. By journaling, you will come to understand your lifestyle habits, stressors, and other factors that contribute to poor physical wellness. You'll also see exactly how much progress you have made, which is very motivating! Your journal will develop over time, depending on your circumstances. An exercise journal can be used to keep track of your:

- Exercise sessions
- Moods
- Sleep
- Eating habits
- Water consumption
- Commitment to your process

I want to add an important note when discussing nutrition. For the six years I was a single parent, I was earning an hourly wage that kept me under the poverty level. I was not able to afford organic food, nor was I able to eat six times a day as I do now. At that time, I had a grocery budget of thirty-five dollars a week for myself and my two daughters. Yes, you read that right. I was not receiving child support, but I did have a full-time job and I worked a lot of overtime. To this day, I am saddened by all the weekends my children spent with babysitters. Thankfully, I learned how to pinch pennies and still eat healthy on a limited budget. I also learned how to use the church's food pantry whenever possible. We always had three healthy meals per day and my girls had snacks in between. There was no junk food because I could not afford it. The highlight of our week was Friday night pizza. I learned that fresh vegetables were cheaper than canned vegetables. And something in the crock pot was cheaper than a four-course meal. I could not afford sauces, gravies, and dressings, so I used spices for flavor. It turns out that's the healthier way, too.

I share this to make the point that my journey evolved over time, and yours will too. Your growth as a person and as a leader will ebb, flow, and be interrupted. That is why it is best to set short-term and long-term goals. We will talk more about goal-setting in upcoming chapters.

Fitness

I embraced my physical wellness journey so passionately that now it is a necessity for me. I am especially drawn to weightlifting because of the focus that it entails with each body part. Weightlifting has been a key factor in my journey by empowering me to release shame and overcome embarrassment about my body. When I was twenty-nine, I became a certified personal trainer and began training fitness clients on the side, in addition to my full-time job. I competed in local bodybuilding shows, and the training, conditioning, and discipline were more healing than I ever imagined. I came to view my introversion as the gift that it was, instead of seeing it as a roadblock. I suddenly felt an inner strength that had previously escaped me, and I built confidence and assertiveness that carried over into my corporate job. At that point, I was managing a small, scrappy team and, although I still had much to learn about people management, it was the beginning of my leadership career.

Fitness is a condition that helps us look, feel, and do our best in our daily activities. It involves the performance of the heart, lungs, and muscles. There are five components that make up physical fitness: cardiorespiratory endurance, muscular strength, muscular endurance, flexibility, and body composition. All five are of equal importance, and together they make up a well-rounded fitness program.

Fitness varies from person to person and is influenced by age, sex, heredity, self-care habits, physical fitness, and eating practices. You cannot do anything about the first three factors. However, it is within your power (and most definitely your responsibility) to change and improve the others if needed. If you are plagued by a stressful work environment, one way you can take control is to work on your fitness. If you are burned-out and unhealthy, then you are not productive, responsive, efficient, or effective.

Excluding one or more of the components of fitness could hinder your results. That does not mean, though, that you must create stress for yourself by jumping into it all at once. It takes time to learn what works for an individual, and even more time to apply it daily. I had no structured exercise in my life until that first day on the exercise bike. I built up slowly, over decades, and now I incorporate about two to three hours of exercise per day into my life. My clients live daily with too little time and too much stress, but as soon as they take one small step towards their physical well-being, they find that the next steps are easier. Now's the time to think about exercise and fitness in your daily life. How do you move your body regularly?

Cardiorespiratory endurance is the ability to burn fat, deliver oxygen and nutrients to tissues, and remove wastes over sustained periods of time. To accomplish this, the heart rate must be elevated within the target zone during exercise. Cardiovascular work is recommended a minimum of three times per week for thirty minutes, and includes a combination of activities, like running, walking, hiking, swimming, and the use of aerobics videos or indoor cardiovascular equipment. Do some research to determine the target heart rate zone for your age.

Muscular strength is the ability of a muscle to exert force for a brief period. This can be combined with muscular endurance, which is the ability of a muscle or group of muscles to sustain repeated contractions, or to continue applying force against a fixed object. Strength training is recommended a minimum of three times per week. Sets, repetitions, and exercises will vary depending on your goals.

With strength training, you can burn body fat, increase bone mass, and shape, tone, or build muscle by using weights. You can lower stress levels, improve eating habits, and ward off osteoporosis. Best of all, strength training can be done with a buddy or in a group and can be relatively inexpensive. All you need is a set or two of handheld weights or large rubber bands.

Flexibility is the ability to move joints and use muscles through their full range of motion. Flexibility training is recommended ten to twelve minutes per day, and it can be incorporated into strength training workouts by stretching between sets. Yoga and Pilates are examples of structured flexibility movement. Many locations offer beginner through advanced classes. This type of flexibility training can also relax the mind, helping you to become more focused and centered. This element of fitness is especially important in the workplace if you are experiencing challenges, roadblocks, or microtraumas.

Body composition is the fifth component of fitness. Body composition refers to the makeup of the body in terms of lean mass and fat mass. It is extremely important to retain as much muscle mass as possible throughout life. Alarmingly, muscle begins to disappear automatically during the aging process, causing a loss of strength, wrinkles, and sagging skin. Thankfully, this impact can be reversed with a proper nutrition and exercise regimen. However, the only way to know if you are gaining or losing muscle mass is with a body composition test. It is a measurement that should be taken periodically when you embark on any fitness program. The loss of lean muscle is a red flag that you are dieting or exercising improperly.

Here's something you might find surprising about body composition: your scale weight does not matter! That is right, it does not matter. What matters is your ratio of fat to lean muscle mass. Though no method is 100 percent accurate, a few of the ways body composition can be tested are by the skin caliper method, underwater hydrostatic weighing, infrared scanner, bioelectrical impedance, or DEXA scan. Some of these tests can be done at your doctor's office or in a lab. Body composition is affected by food and water intake, illness, stress, sodium, medications, menstrual cycles, lack of sleep, and many other factors. It is only a guideline, and it can vary by the day.

Fitness experts set acceptable body fat ranges of 18–20 percent for women under forty, 13–16 percent for men under forty, 23–27 percent for women forty to sixty-plus, and 19–20 percent for men forty to sixty-plus.

Developing Your Ideal Exercise Program

How often, how long, and how hard you exercise, and what kinds of exercises you do, should be determined by what you are trying to accomplish. Some of the factors to be considered are your goals, your present fitness level, your age, health, skills, interests, cost, and convenience. For example, an athlete training for a high-level competition would follow a different program than a person whose goals are good health and the ability to meet work and recreational needs. When developing an exercise routine, ask yourself: What is the best time of day to exercise? Then make an appointment with yourself. Will you be more committed to your routine if you have a workout buddy? If so, choose someone with like goals and a similar schedule. That way, you can work out together and keep each other motivated.

Your exercise program should include something from each of the five physical fitness components described previously. Each workout should begin with a warm-up and end with a cool-down. As a rule, unless you are a seasoned athlete, you should space your workouts throughout the week and avoid consecutive days of hard exercise. The body needs time to recover.

Always consult your physician before beginning any new exercise program. Then start out slow so you do not overdo it. Exercise helps build a strong foundation for your body and will help you recover faster from stress, injury, and medical conditions.

When I was forty-four, I had my thyroid removed and was also diagnosed with an autoimmune disorder. Both conditions are characterized by severe weight gain, body aches, joint pain, and depression. I was devastated by the news, but continued my exercise regimen, sometimes literally forcing myself to the gym. I knew that if I let go of that daily habit, it would not only impact me physically but would also increase my cPTSD symptoms. My discipline has paid off in that I have been able to overcome, and in some cases, even avoid, many of the debilitating symptoms that render some people with autoimmune disorders unable to function.

When I am coaching my clients, they inevitably bring up the topic of exercise and realize that they need to incorporate more of it into their life. They realize that poor physical wellness is causing them to mismanage their communication, emotions, and stress levels, and this is impacting their performance. As an executive coach, I cannot offer advice or consultative direction, but I can help clients determine what kind of fitness works for them, how to get started, and how to set a better example for their team. They usually see immediate results in one form or another, but they need to take small steps and work it into their schedule. For many years, I worked out daily but never set foot in a gym, because I had small children and a packed schedule. So I created my own convenient home gym with various pieces of equipment. Finally, when I started competing, I enrolled in a gym, but by then my kids were older and my schedule was more manageable. The great thing about exercise is that you can customize it to fit your lifestyle and schedule.

Healthy Eating Habits

But exercise alone won't make lasting changes in your work life or leadership abilities. Exercise and healthy eating habits can keep you focused at work by eliminating brain fog, give you the stamina needed for tough problem-solving, and keep you on your game when delivering constructive feedback. The various components of fitness work in conjunction with proper nutrition to ensure that your body receives adequate calories daily. As you burn calories during exercise, it is important to replace those calories in ways that meet your fitness goals. The number of calories to consume daily will vary for each person, and it will *always* depend on that person's activity level.

Intuitive eating is a philosophy of learning to listen to your body as far as the amount, frequency, and timing of your food intake. In this way, there is a mind/body connection and a total awareness of what your body needs. This typically means eating about four to six meals per day, one serving of each food. However, some people might find that one serving is too much or too little. Aside from the factors just mentioned, determining your portion sizes depends on only one thing—eating until you are satisfied, not full. This means you must eat mindfully, and you may have to measure portions for the first week or two just to get a frame of reference for portion sizes.

Intuitive eating means having a lot of food on hand. How do you plan for that? Do you grocery-shop once a week? If not, you will need to start. Another big mistake people make is not scheduling a regular shopping day. Without healthy foods on hand, most people will opt for eating out. When you shop, be sure to choose a combination of protein, carbohydrates, fruits, and veggies.

One downside to eating so frequently is that it can mean a lot of cooking, which can be time-consuming. This is easily resolved by spending one or two hours cooking in advance. Many people tend to do this on weekends. For instance, they will cook large pots of rice and oatmeal, bake several potatoes, and grill a week's worth of meat. This way, there is always food on hand for each meal. My clients initially tell me that they have no time to shop or cook healthy. But they soon realize that they can make time for the things that are a priority—it can be done. This is especially important because poor nutrition impacts your mental capacity at work. If you are not eating properly, you are not on top of things in the office, cannot manage crises, and cannot pivot in an agile way in fast-paced work environments. You have no resilience.

The components of a healthy and balanced diet Include:

- A combination of all basic food groups and fresh water.
- Nutrition that is free from pesticides and chemicals.
- The correct number of calories for your body type and activity level.
- Nutrition that is "clean," or in its most natural form and minimally processed. "Clean eating" refers to eating a diet low in processed foods. In an ideal world, this would

mean home-cooked foods that are fresh, organic, and a combination of all the basic food groups.

- Nutrition that supports your fitness goals, medical issues, and philosophy.

Nutrition is a component of physical wellness that is well within your control. In times of high stress due to life's challenges, the body releases hormones that can contribute to increased body fat. That in turn can cause fatigue, a slow metabolism, and an unhealthy digestive system. Your body needs healthy food and plenty of it to reverse the effects of stress. Focusing on small, frequent meals keeps adequate calories in the body.

When you restrict calories by not eating, your body refuses to give up the extra body fat. So you must give your body what it wants, and it will burn calories more efficiently. By eating this way, you will also keep your energy level high all day. No more midday fatigue in the office or having your eyes go blurry at the computer. That is the crash you feel when your blood sugar dips too low.

One of my clients always felt on edge, impatient, and frustrated in her morning meetings. As we unpacked the situation in coaching, she admitted that she was not eating breakfast. She agreed to try an experiment of eating a small breakfast each day for one week. At our next session, she reported back with the results. She claimed to feel calmer, more alert, and more engaged in meetings. You may not realize it, but food also affects your mood. When you do not eat, or when you do not eat healthy foods, your mood changes drastically. That is your body trying desperately to tell you something.

Try a similar experiment the next time you are in a bad mood. Take notice of your mood and then eat a healthy snack. Check your mood again in about twenty minutes. You will find that it has improved, and possibly some of your physical symptoms have disappeared too.

To improve your nutrition, you can begin by cleaning out your cupboards. Toss foods that are high in sugar or highly processed. Become accustomed to choosing healthier foods at the grocery store. You will need to combine healthy eating practices with a stable exercise plan if you want your body to respond properly.

Water is an often-forgotten component of nutrition. Water intake is critical, and when you design your customized nutrition plan, you will follow a formula to help you determine your daily water intake. Here are some important things to know about water:

- Water helps flush impurities out of the body
- By the time you get thirsty, you are already dehydrating
- Water increases your metabolic rate by forcing the kidneys to work harder
- Water contributes to healthy skin, hair, and nails

The chart below is a simple explanation of the basic food groups:

(COMPLETE) PROTEIN *A complete protein includes all nine amino acids that we cannot synthesize ourselves	Feeds the muscles: egg whites, lean red meat, poultry, fish
COMPLEX CARBOHYDRATES	Give the body sugar to burn during activity: whole grains, oats, rice (the darker the better)

Unsaturated Fats	Supply energy, support healthy skin and nails, and lubricate joints and ligaments. Olive oil, almond oil, flax oil, sunflower oil, nuts/seeds
Fibrous Carbohydrates (veggies) **Simple Carbohydrates (fruit)**	Supply vitamins, minerals, and fiber. They burn differently than complex carbohydrates

Environmental Factors

Stress, lack of sleep, pollution, and hormonal changes all impact the body, and work performance. As a leader, your physical wellness is paramount in the workplace because it gives you the stamina and resilience to focus and manage the stress of your job.

It is impossible to avoid stress and environmental toxins, but you can do your best to educate yourself and be aware of what they are and what they do to you. You can reduce emotional stress in the workplace by upgrading your lifestyle, slowing down, and relaxing more. Here are some self-care suggestions that we will discuss in more detail when we address the other dimensions of wellness:

- Do yoga
- Read
- Walk
- Enjoy nature
- Nap
- Get together with family (unless that is too stressful)
- Do whatever is fun for you
- Get more sleep

You can reduce environmental toxins by:

- Being conscious of the environment
- Aligning your lifestyle with your values regarding the environment
- Breathing clean or filtered air whenever possible
- Staying in a smoke-free environment
- Eating toxin-free food
- Avoiding the consumption of toxins like drugs, caffeine, alcohol, or excess sugar
- Doing your part to control pollution and littering

When your body is "clean" and toxin-free, it can let its guard down. There is no need for it to protect itself from toxins. It will then function more efficiently and effectively and will let go of excess protective body fat. Take an assessment of what is around you that is toxic. This will be a long journey, so keep it manageable and try to eliminate those things little by little.

Experiment, but Not to the Extreme

Nutrition is extraordinarily complex, and each body responds differently to various food combinations. You will need to experiment a bit to find what works for you. Remember, do not eliminate important nutrients from your diet—you can upset the body's delicate balance. You can easily throw off hormone and other chemical levels that are crucial to the body's functioning. These hormones keep you going during a midday meeting, or help you pay attention during a long Zoom session.

So be cautious of extreme eating patterns or fad diets. If you notice any of the red flags below, or other things that seem highly unusual for your body, seek advice from your doctor, an experienced fitness trainer, or both. One tool that will help you notice these red flags is your fitness journal. If you are consistently tracking and documenting your eating, workouts, moods, and other habits, it will not take long to notice when something is out of the ordinary. Looking back at your journal will help you immediately assess the cause of any problems. Some red flags for unhealthy eating patterns are:

- Low energy levels
- Loss of strength
- Loss of lean muscle
- Insomnia
- Fluctuating moods
- Lack of focus
- Blood pressure and cholesterol issues
- Frequent illness

Incorporating Medical Exams

Always be sure to keep up on your routine physical exams, because that is another way to track what is happening to your body. Luckily, I have always been very proactive about my medical checkups because, as a trauma survivor, I tend to hold my stress in my physical body. To this day, I incorporate various trauma release practices into my daily life to try to reduce the physical impact of past trauma on my body. In addition to exercise, a few of my trauma release practices include breathwork, a practice called Trauma Release Exercises (TRE), meditation, yoga, visual journaling, tapping, and desire mapping.

However, at age twenty-eight, the stress of the workplace and of single parenthood led to a diagnosis of Temporomandibular Joint

Dysfunction (TMJ). I was terrified when the symptoms first occurred. I was a single parent, working, going to school, and trying to survive. Then my jaw started locking up on the left side. I could only open my mouth a few millimeters. After a few minutes of hot compresses, my jaw would release and open. This started happening more and more frequently until, finally, one day my jaw locked and never opened. I had what the doctors called a "closed lock." Apparently, some people have an "open lock" where their jaw locks in the open position. I stayed in a closed lock for six months. I could still work, speak, squeeze in a toothbrush, and smile. But eating became too difficult, and I had to use a straw. After seeing many doctors, trying various modalities, and losing ten pounds, I finally had surgery.

The surgery was a success, but the doctor said that my stress level needed to be reduced or the same thing would happen on the right side. Exercise and journaling, another practice that always seemed to calm me, was not enough. The doctor's comment was a stark realization that I needed to up my game and do better at caring for myself.

That six months and recovery from surgery derailed me from my lifeline of exercise. You will be derailed too, at times. There will always be challenges that make it difficult to stick to your eating and workout routine. Travel, holidays, illness, and other life events will throw you off your schedule. However, with a little planning and creative thinking, you can minimize some of these challenges, like travel and holidays.

Staying Healthy during Travel and Holidays

Business and personal travel can take its toll physically, mentally, and emotionally. All-day meetings, late dinners, lack of sleep, no time to call home, and crowded airports all add to stress levels. Does frequent traveling make it hard for you to take care of yourself? If so, you're not alone. Now, learn to take some steps to proactively plan how to better deal with stress during your next trip.

Decide prior to your trip that you will be exercising. Pack the appropriate clothing and decide how you will fit it into your schedule. Will you need to get up a bit earlier? Can you allow a midday workout to take priority over socializing with coworkers? Do you know ahead of time what your workout routine will be so that you can maximize efficiency in the fitness center? Can you work out in your hotel room, or does the hotel have a fitness center? Simple advance planning will help you answer these questions. Depending on your travel and work schedule, you may be able to squeeze in a workout first thing in the morning. Or you may find time to do a quick, no-sweat midday routine. For some, a workout feels best after a long, stressful day. Either way, it just takes some advance planning and prioritizing. It is possible to spend less than an hour working out, yet you will feel the benefits all day long.

Case Study

One of my clients, Phil, was so pressed for time while on business trips that we devised a workout he could do right in his hotel room, first thing in the morning. He packed a jump rope and resistance bands, and had a streaming yoga video on his phone. He was able to work out thirty to forty-five minutes each morning and, one morning, he even modified the workout to twenty minutes. He reported feeling more energetic during the day, in a better mood, and had a higher confidence level. You can experience the same results too, with some advance planning.

Exercising on the road has many benefits. You will sleep better, feel more relaxed, and be less irritable. Exercise helps reduce fatigue and stiff muscles due to travel. It will also clear your head, allowing you to conduct business much more successfully. You will even notice less weight gain after a trip.

Many frequent travelers also find it challenging to eat properly while away from home and develop unhealthy eating habits when on the road. Here are some tips and tricks my frequent-flyer clients have developed to reverse those unhealthy habits. Whether traveling by car or plane, always keep healthy snacks with you. Granola bars, homemade trail mix, protein or cereal bars, nuts, fruit, or a pre-made salad are great options.

Restaurants are also very accommodating when it comes to special orders. You can ask to have vegetables grilled instead of cooked in butter. Or you can request to have sauces, gravies, or dressings served on the side. When browsing the dessert menu, consider sherbet, frozen yogurt, or something similarly low in fat. Ask for substitutes like salad in place of usthh fries, or fruit instead of onion rings. Many restaurants offer a lite menu with tasty low-fat choices. But there is no reason to eliminate the higher-calorie foods; just keep moderation in mind. If you are planning to stay in a hotel while traveling, be sure to request a refrigerator and microwave for your room. That way it is easier to plan healthy meals or snacks.

Another challenge is controlling eating during the holidays or during events. These tips and tricks may help you out:

- When hosting a party, be sure to include some healthy choices so that you have options. Better yet, include only healthy foods.

- If you are cooking for your guests, use healthy recipes or healthy substitutes in your recipes.

- Keep moderation in mind.
- Limit or eliminate alcohol, and drink water instead. Put fruit in your water for added flavor.
- If you do drink alcohol, then drink plenty of water throughout the night to keep from dehydrating.
- Be sure to eat a full meal before you attend an event. You will be less hungry and have more willpower.
- Do not go hungry all day to save room for party food. This is a poor decision, and you will eat yourself into oblivion.

The Self-Care Component

Physical wellness can be used to combat stress, workplace challenges, trauma, and health issues. It was the first step on my journey. Creating a strong foundation of complete physical wellness through exercising, nutrition, and self-care has a ripple effect on your body. It also helps you to set a good example as a leader for your coworkers. If your coworkers see you practicing self-care by taking a snack break, taking sick days when you're ill, or walking around the block during their lunch hour, they may also want to make positive changes to their self-care regimen. Self-care is an important area of physical wellness that is often overlooked, but it can help you build confidence and self-esteem. I am introducing the topic of self-care here, but it is so critical that you will also read about it in a few of the other chapters.

How do you honor and acknowledge yourself? Self-care is a combination of activities that you choose to do daily, if possible, because they are fun and make you feel good about yourself. Sometimes I refer to these rituals as a self-care affair.

These activities keep you present and mindful because, when you perform them, you are paying close attention to yourself. A form of embodiment practice, self-care can ground you, reduce anxiety, and offer many mental health benefits.

Pampering yourself could include reading your favorite book, taking a nap, talking with a friend, or meditating. Daily pampering makes all the difference in the world during times of chaos or transition. And it should become just as important as regular exercise and proper nutrition. Sometimes self-care becomes an action item for my busy executive leaders who struggle with making time for themselves.

The dimension of physical wellness can be used as a self-help tool, or buffer, for those experiencing stress and trauma in the workplace. When we are facing daily conflict or huge decisions at work, we tend to forget about good health. So stress gets the best of us and creates a nasty cycle of self-abuse.

Case Study

The shift toward physical wellness is not impossible. Let me tell you about Kim, one of my clients who did it. Kim was overweight, diagnosed with adrenal fatigue, not sleeping, had no energy, felt no motivation, and was chronically depressed. She was not having any fun in her life because all she did was work and work more once she got home. Her relationships were suffering at work and in her personal life. She was a senior vice president, but no one took her seriously and she was not accomplishing her strategic goals. Her negativity was contagious, plus she suffered from impostor syndrome, which we will discuss in later chapters. This all impacted her productivity and that of her team. They were not meeting deadlines; they were not motivated, creative, or innovative. Kim worked on her physical wellness in coaching and noticed an immediate shift! She started sleeping better, had more energy, her mood improved, and she made more time for herself. She even started losing weight. All of this helped her adrenal fatigue and negativity. My point is that if Kim can do it, anyone can do it.

Kim started slowly, and you can too. Realize that it is a process that will improve over time. So be gentle with yourself. You might want to begin by assessing your lifestyle and personal habits in your fitness journal. You know, intuitively, what steps you need to take, and journaling will validate that for you. Surround yourself with plenty of support.

Physical Wellness Is a Choice and Responsibility

Being consistently dedicated to your physical wellness is a choice and a responsibility. It will allow you to reap several benefits, including lower stress levels and a healthier body. Improving physical wellness will help you focus on yourself, building confidence and self-esteem.

I always get the same question from my clients—what does physical wellness have to do with leadership? It has everything to do with leadership. Your journey as a human being will influence everyone in your path. Your journey as a leader will influence everyone in your organization and on your team. It is your responsibility to set a good example for those people, just as it is your responsibility to handle your past trauma, your current trauma, and your workplace challenges. If a leader is burned-out and unhealthy, they are not productive, responsive, efficient, effective, or leading by example. If this is you, then you are also not communicating appropriately, managing your emotions, handling your stress, or able to pivot in an agile way when needed. You are not on top of things, nor are you resilient and able to handle crises when they occur. Improving your physical wellness will shift the scale (no pun intended) in your favor and give you more influence and presence.

Summary

- If you are burned-out and unhealthy, then you cannot lead and could possibly even contribute to the dysfunctional culture of the workplace.

- You owe it to yourself and your team to lead from a place of peak performance and to set the highest example.

- Physical wellness is an important component of the Eight Dimensions of Wellness model.

- Physical wellness consists of fitness, nutrition, and self-care.

- Fitness consists of strength, cardiovascular, and flexibility training.

- Nutrition involves food, water, meal planning, environmental factors, and supplementation.

- Things like holidays and travel can throw off your routine, so use your journal, meal plan, support system, and other tools to get you back on track.

- Self-care relates to the many things you can do to treat yourself well.

PHYSICAL WELLNESS 43

ACTION ITEM

Before moving on to the next chapter, please complete the following exercise:

- Choose a journal and begin tracking or writing for five minutes a day

Chapter 2

INTELLECTUAL WELLNESS

Within the first pillar of transforming yourself is the second dimension of wellness: intellectual wellness. Everyone's journey across these dimensions begins at a different place and progresses at a different pace. Therefore, the order of the dimensions is of less importance than your actual journey. You also may fluctuate back and forth between dimensions, since growth is not linear.

It has often been said that knowledge is power. I prefer to say that knowledge is empowerment. I consider myself a lifelong learner, and by continuously increasing my intellectual wellness, I have also increased my confidence and self-esteem. Focusing on your intellectual wellness relates to the continuous acquisition of knowledge, awareness of current events, and your expression of creativity. Intellectual wellness also relates to identifying any gaps in your knowledge and filling those gaps by exploring your interests and applying your unique style of learning to your personal and professional life.

While knowledge absolutely helps you stay relevant in your career, it serves a more critical role with regard to your personal development. I will address both topics in this chapter, plus provide you with the process and tools to continuously improve your intellectual wellness. Success in your life, mastering challenges, and overcoming trauma all start with your own personal growth. Intellectual growth is part of that imperative growth, just like physical wellness. Before you can successfully improve the intellectual gaps in your professional life, you must first master knowledge gaps in your personal life. You do this by learning about yourself, your environment, and your community.

How can you be successful in your career if you lead an unfulfilled personal life? Are you aware of what is happening in your world? Do you know your larger purpose, or what impact you want to have on others? If you cannot answer those questions yet, do not worry—we will discuss your purpose and your mission statement in a later chapter. But what you can focus on now is this: it will benefit you as a leader if you have a well-rounded knowledge base.

If you lead a team, you surely have experienced being faced with an array of interactions with your direct reports daily. They have needs that are not being met, personal or health challenges, and disagreements with coworkers. They may come to you with topics that seemingly have nothing to do with work, yet these things impact their productivity. They expect support, and it is your responsibility to be a resource for them. While it is easy, and at times appropriate, to refer them to Human Resources or to the company Employee Assistance Program, you need to do better as a leader.

The way to better address the concerns of your team is to arm yourself with knowledge, a broad perspective, and an open and creative mind. Be curious about your own thought processes and learn about yourself. Reading this book is one way to do that, but there are other ways too. Surround yourself with people you can learn from, seek opinions of, and initiate discussions with—in other words, broaden your social connections. Explore your actions, thoughts, and triggers. Develop curiosity about why you do things, why others do things, and how that behavior impacts others.

Embark on informal learning through podcasts, reading, workbooks, or workshops. Perhaps take part in formal learning, like a certificate or degree program. What is it you want to learn about? Your learning benefits everyone with whom you engage. The more you know, the more you can offer in advice or referrals to various resources. I am not suggesting that you become a walking encyclopedia. Your learning must be based on things in which you are genuinely interested.

Exploring your creative side is also a way to enhance your intellectual wellness. If you had the time, what would you like to create? Perhaps you would create a book, poem, dance, song, piece of art, piece of clothing, speech, or side business. There are infinite ways to express creativity that all relate to increasing your intellectual wellness. This is such a critical part of your development as a human being. You can extend your curious mind to learning about current events, world events, and social justice by subscribing to a newspaper or magazine, or committing to listening to the news a few times a week. Any of these actions will help you become more interested in the world around you, develop more empathy, and be more open-minded and understanding of the plights of others.

Case Study

My client John managed a team of five direct reports. Through biweekly one-to-ones, John knew that one person on his team, Sue, had a challenging medical problem. Sue shared this information with him when discussing her stress level and work-life balance. Fortunately, John had a broad medical knowledge base and had dealt with certain medical issues himself. He had recently read an article about a local medical clinic that had implemented alternative treatment methods for certain diagnoses. When he mentioned this to Sue, she checked into it and discovered some new options for treating her illness.

I used to think that having knowledge about various topics meant that you also had to form an opinion on all those topics. Well, that would be exhausting and overwhelming. Now, I am perfectly comfortable not having an opinion on everything and simply learning and observing. As a matter of fact, having too many opinions can be detrimental to you and those with whom you interact. Sometimes, what is necessary is to observe, learn, and gain knowledge, but not make an evaluation or form an opinion. If you genuinely want to lead with passion and influence, it is important at times for you to present various options and leave it to others to decide upon the best solution for themselves and their unique situation. However, if you do need to present the options along with the solution, you will be in a great position to do that also. But without knowledge about yourself and the world around you, you cannot do either.

So, focus first on growing your personal knowledge and then work to improve your professional knowledge. My learning stopped at age sixteen when I got married and dropped out of the tenth grade. Life during that first marriage was a continuation of the survival mode I had become accustomed to while growing up. My only objective was to navigate being in a dysfunctional marriage that involved my husband's criminal behavior, legal proceedings, substance abuse, poverty, control, abuse, and oppression. To this day, I am grateful for taking the high school equivalency exam and obtaining my GED. That was the only way I could enter college later in life, and it was the first step along my path of intellectual wellness.

A few years after my divorce, when my children were still toddlers, I took an interest in psychology. I explored the topic further by talking to a college guidance counselor. What started as an idea to take one psychology class to enhance my personal intellect ended up with me enrolling in a business bachelor's program. Psychology was one of the electives offered. This was the beginning of my growth spurt in intellectual wellness, which, in this case, expanded both my personal and professional intellect. In all honesty, that business program was a painful pursuit due to everything else on my plate. And though I had to make some adjustments, I obtained a college degree.

By the time of my enrollment, my children and I were living in subsidized housing while I worked full-time plus overtime. I was exhausted daily, trying to exercise and trying to navigate single parenthood without financial help. But I was desperate to improve my knowledge and skills to make more money so that the three of us could survive. Plus, I realized that I had a genuine interest in the business world. However, halfway through my four-year program, I became extremely ill. I was constantly sick with upper respiratory issues, the flu, colds, and exhaustion. I finally decided to take a few semesters off to get my health in order. Once I physically recovered, I switched my bachelor's program to an associate's program. That adjustment removed a lot of pressure from me. I did not want to abandon the program altogether, so I settled for a lesser goal with the intent of going back later for my bachelor's degree.

Those of you who have gone to school while working and raising children, being a single parent, and experiencing financial challenges or medical and mental health struggles might understand why I say it was a painful pursuit. Nonetheless, I am glad I did it, because it elevated my role at work from an individual contributor to a team leader with ten direct reports. But, at that time, I was far from a good leader because I had no support, no direction, and no guidance. I was also slowly realizing that dysfunction was everywhere in the workplace and that I was spinning my wheels in a broken system.

I intuitively knew that arming myself with personal and professional knowledge would help me succeed. I continued expanding my personal knowledge base through reading, self-study, and attending personal growth workshops.

Later, in my thirties and forties, I earned a bachelor's of science in management degree and a master's of science in industrial and organizational psychology. I continued to assess my gaps and enhance my professional learning by earning six business certifications. My clients also realize the importance of improving their professional skills to stay relevant in their industry. Phil, who was mentioned in Chapter One, sought out coaching so that he could achieve a promotion in his field of Information Technology (IT). One certification was all he needed, and he obtained it in two months, securing that promotion!

Let me take a pause here to highlight an important point. Working on personal and professional intellectual wellness is not a linear process. You do not necessarily have to work on your personal area before you can address the professional area. You can do both simultaneously, but it takes discipline and structure. For the purpose of this book and the eight dimensions, the concept is to work on yourself first, and then integrate that growth into the other parts of your life. Realistically, it cannot always happen that way, nor does it need to. But for those of you who are new to this concept, I recommend starting with your own growth and then integrating it into other areas. This book is set up in that exact fashion, but as you get more skilled with growth, you will see how easy it is to do this work simultaneously.

To improve professional intellectual wellness, you must again know and explore your interests, but you must also identify knowledge gaps that might be holding you back in your role. Gaps are those areas where you need to grow professionally, areas where you are challenged, or areas where you are stuck. For some people, knowledge gaps are minimal and can be easily rectified with coaching or mentoring. As an example, let us look at Ben's situation.

Case Study

Ben was a senior manager in a financial institution, and his goal was to advance to a director position within one year. Ben knew that, in his organization, as in most organizations, promotions are seldom guaranteed. But he wanted to position himself in such a way that he could build a good business case for a promotion if the opportunity arose. Ben knew that he hated conflict and did not handle difficult conversations with ease. That was a knowledge gap for him, and if he ever wanted to progress to the next role, he needed to be more direct and assertive when handling conflict. In coaching, we unpacked previous situations where he could have been more assertive, and we role-played upcoming situations and ways to disarm potential conflict.

In Ben's case, his knowledge gap was related to a soft skill, but people also have knowledge gaps related to technical skills. Soft skills are also known as people skills, or the interpersonal skills related to interacting with others. One way to identify knowledge gaps is with a little self-awareness. People intuitively know their deficits because they feel uncomfortable in those areas. Whether it is public speaking, communication, time management, engaging others, running meetings, staying focused, work-life balance, or collaboration, you can most likely pinpoint the area(s) where you need to improve to be successful in this role or in the next one.

Sometimes you can determine your own gaps, but another way to identify them is by requesting feedback from your coworkers or other people in your daily life, like friends and even family. Although it may be intimidating at first to ask others for feedback, it's important for your professional and personal growth. Many companies offer 360 assessments or other tools that you can send out to collect anonymous feedback from groups of people. If there is no formal process in place at your organization, you can develop your own informal way to request coworker feedback.

Your manager should also give you consistent feedback so that you always know where you stand. This is a drastic oversight in most companies, because many managers do not give reliable, adequate, or frequent feedback. The reason can be because they do not know how, do not want to, feel as though they do not have the time to, or purposely withhold feedback to control others. The latter is considered a form of microtrauma and can leave direct reports feeling confused and submerged in self-doubt. Another form of microtrauma is when a manager only provides negative or critical feedback and never any positive feedback. People need both to learn and grow, and it is a manager's job to support the growth of their direct reports. Feedback helps a person understand their knowledge gaps so that they can create strategies to improve. As a bonus, it will help your team's growth and production.

Ideally, you will have feedback through your own self-awareness, and from your manager and your coworkers, to understand your professional gaps and build a strategy. If you are not getting feedback, it is up to you to make the request to whomever you want feedback from, because you must take ownership of your growth. Assuming you do receive consistent feedback, it is also up to you to figure out what to do about it. My clients and I spend many sessions debriefing feedback they have received from their manager and coworkers. Typically, the more senior the role, the more often the gaps are related to a lack of soft skills. The lower-level roles will more likely have gaps related to technical skills.

Some strategies you can use to address knowledge gaps include professional development training, formal education, being mentored, being coached, reading more, role-playing new skills, practicing new skills in real time at work and in meetings, and shadowing others to learn technical skills. Strategies can be as simple as listening to podcasts, or more formal options like taking a class. The appropriate strategy should always match the gap, and all the strategies should be documented in a tool called a personal learning plan (PLP). This is different than an individual development plan (IDP). Contrary to common belief, neither tool is remedial. Both tools are strictly for the tracking of your goals and strategies. You can choose to share each with your manager, but it is not mandatory.

If you want to become a true resource to your team and others in your sphere of influence, it is critical for you to address your intellectual wellness from both personal and professional angles. The PLP is a tool that allows you to think through and document your learning, or strategies, for the year. You can list the gaps to be addressed, your strategies or the learning programs you will undertake, the length of each program, and deadlines to complete them. Develop the mindset of continuous learning and update your PLP at the end of each year for the upcoming year.

Now, you are probably wondering how to fit this learning into your busy schedule. That process will be different for everyone. Your learning may need to be physically scheduled into your calendar. Your learning plan is not a document to fill out and then forget about—you must schedule the time to execute it.

The resource library is another tool you can create to save valuable articles, links to interesting topics, and any other resources that you have come across as you begin educating yourself. The reason to collect this information is not only for your own reference, but also to help your team, coworkers, peers, or others, should they need information. Part of your role as a leader is to help others grow and to be a resource yourself when others are in need. You are not expected to have all the answers, but you are expected to do more than just refer them to Human Resources. Having a collection of resources positions you to assist in the best way possible. As a coach, working with executives from more than twenty industries and in roles from manager up to the C-suite, I now have a resource library with hundreds of links on topics from A to Z.

Summary

- Improving intellectual wellness involves addressing the gaps in your personal and professional knowledge base

- It's critical to seek feedback from others, create a plan, and make time to execute on the plan

- Improving your intellectual wellness allows you to empower yourself and others

ACTION ITEMS

Before moving on to the next chapter, please complete the following exercises:

- Proactively identify your knowledge gaps and create a PLP using your own self-awareness and feedback from others
- Block out time in your calendar to execute on your learning plan for the year
- Create a resource library tool with links and resources that you find valuable

Chapter 3

EMOTIONAL WELLNESS

Of all eight dimensions, my emotional wellness has been the most severely impacted by my childhood trauma. Many of my childhood memories were repressed until I was in my thirties. However, I did remember the devastation of my mother being killed in a somewhat mysterious one-car crash on a sunny summer day when I was seven. Those fragmented memories floated in and out—the police coming to my house, being told at my mom's funeral not to cry because "big girls don't cry," not being allowed to ever speak of her again, her clothes being burned in a backyard bonfire, and being suddenly cut off from her side of the family.

Then there was the memory, during the same summer, of my two-year-old disabled brother being permanently institutionalized even though my mother's family begged to care for him. Another sketchy memory from yet the same summer was of my near-drowning accident and my wish that I had died rather than be saved. There was a lot of devastation and a lot of loss for me in just one summer. But it almost pales in comparison to the hell that ensued in my sociopathic household after my mother's death. I remember being deeply depressed and withdrawn, and having daily headaches and stomachaches. My low weight was most likely caused by being sent to bed with no dinner if I did something deemed "wrong." The abuse, violence, and neglect left me feeling confused, shamed, abandoned, and longing for my mother. As an introvert and HSP, I went deeper into myself and found ways to survive that included simply repressing the memories. Since HSPs are more sensitive to their environment, they are also more sensitive to trauma. My traumatic experiences continued in my first marriage and throughout my divorce, which involved stalking, harassment, and threats to kidnap my children. Though single parenting carried its own type of stress, it gave me somewhat of a reprieve from the abusive control of others who had dictated my life.

The panic attacks started shortly after my second marriage began. Being a single parent for six years, I had been mostly in survival mode. But, at age twenty-nine, I remarried, and life eased up a bit for myself and my daughters. We adjusted to having a two-income family, a bigger house, a dog, and a cat. I felt happy and nurtured for the first time in years. The first two years of that marriage were pretty stress-free, until my repressed memories started to resurface. Therapists have told me that sometimes trauma memories start to show up during a time in life when we feel safe and loved. The first panic attack happened while I was driving, and I had to pull over. I had eaten and slept well, so I could not understand the dizziness. Even harder to understand was the fear that gripped me from head to toe, the hyperventilating, and the temporary paralysis I experienced while I sat in my car. The episodes repeated themselves multiple times over weeks and months, even while I slept. I got in to see a therapist, and only then, when my episodes were identified as panic attacks, did I begin working on the trauma of losing my mother. Little did I know at the time that many more trauma memories would be revealed over the coming decades, and that I would eventually be diagnosed with cPTSD.

Emotional wellness involves the ability to successfully handle life's stresses and adapt to change and difficult times. Being emotionally and mentally well allows you to make healthy personal choices, express and manage your feelings effectively, and accept your own feelings and those of others. It involves the application of stress management, relaxation techniques, self-awareness, and acceptance. My emotional wellness had been short-circuited by my childhood trauma. Research has proven that repeated childhood trauma can alter a child's nervous system, and even their DNA. It is the same for children who grow up in poverty or other debilitating environments.

Traumatic experiences impact emotions both in the moment and over the long term. According to Seth J. Gillihan, PhD, in an article in *Psychology Today*, "Whatever the source, trauma leaves its imprint on the brain."[1] For example, a study published in *Neuroscience and Biobehavioral Reviews*[2] found a link between PTSD and greater brain activity in areas that process fear. According to Psychiatry.org,[3] people with PTSD have intense, disturbing thoughts and feelings related to their experience that last long after the traumatic event has ended. The workplace is filled with employees who have unresolved trauma, and they are trying to lead, work with customers, and be productive corporate citizens. This is the reason why every one of us has a critical responsibility to take care of ourselves, to heal, to identify traumatic environments, and to arm ourselves with the tools to do so. We must break the cycle of trauma in the home, the workplace, and the community, not only to heal ourselves but to also empower others.

Unfortunately, my emotional wellness took another hit throughout my corporate career. During my career, I have been verbally assaulted, physically barred from leaving my office, cursed at, threatened, and subjected to displays of physical outrage. All

---

[1] Gillihan, Seth J. "21 Common Reactions to Trauma." *Psychology Today*. September 7, 2016. https://www.psychologytoday.com/us/blog/think-act-be/201609/21-common-reactions-trauma.

[2] Sherin, Jonathan E, and Charles B Nemeroff. 2011. "Post-Traumatic Stress Disorder: The Neurobiological Impact of Psychological Trauma." *Dialogues in Clinical Neuroscience* 13 (3): 263–78. https://www.ncbi.nlm.nih.gov/pmc/articles/PMC3182008/.

[3] American Psychiatric Association. 2022. "What Is Posttraumatic Stress Disorder (PTSD)?" Psychiatry.org. American Psychiatric Association. November 2022. https://www.psychiatry.org/patients-families/ptsd/what-is-ptsd.

these incidents happened within a corporate setting, and each time the perpetrator was either a peer or a senior manager. One of the perpetrators even worked in the human resources department. As terrified as I was, I filed complaints each time, cooperated in the investigations, and followed through until things were resolved. It was critical for me to use my voice, which I could not do as a child.

My emotional well-being has been challenged since childhood, but I have adopted tools and techniques to build resilience. Many of my clients either have experienced childhood trauma, are currently the victims of workplace microtrauma, or have direct reports and peers who are suffering in that way. Our experiences shape our thoughts, emotions, and behaviors, which unfortunately influence workplace culture. Over 90 percent of my clients work with me in coaching sessions to learn how to better manage their emotions. Either they are self-aware enough to understand that this is a knowledge gap for them, or they have received feedback that tells them so.

One of the core competencies of a skillful leader is emotional agility—the ability to be aware of one's inner world, pivot with life's challenges, and recognize and manage unhealthy emotions productively. It is vitally important to be aware of emotions, but not be controlled by them. It is equally important to not stuff emotions down. Instead, you need to learn what to do with them, and how to leverage them at the appropriate times. Here, I will share techniques that have helped me improve my emotional wellness and become more grounded. I will also share strategies that have helped my clients survive, and even thrive, in the workplace.

My clients do not know where to start when they bring up this issue in coaching. They describe being overtaken, at times, by anger, frustration, fear, anxiety, stress, and the pressures of their role. In the workplace, they are unable to hide their physical reactions, make inappropriate verbal responses, feel either disconnected from others or too caught up in drama, cannot diffuse intense situations, and cannot lead with true executive presence. These leaders are one hundred percent controlled by their emotions and, even worse, are setting this example for their direct reports.

Case Study

Abby was a senior director in a healthcare facility and described herself as someone with a short fuse and little patience. In meetings, Abby frequently became impatient, interrupted people, and used rude language. She received this feedback from her peers and her manager but did not know what to do about it. In coaching, she explained that she was able to resolve issues quickly in her mind and got annoyed when the rest of the group kept brainstorming for the answer. So she would get impatient, interrupt, and dictate the solution and next steps to the group. This came across as horribly abrasive to the meeting attendees and made her direct reports feel as though their opinions weren't valued. Abby's emotions were getting the best of her, and, in coaching, we worked on developing her empathy and listening skills. Once she started listening more in meetings, and asking more open-ended questions, she had a better understanding of where others were in their thinking process. She also realized that by jumping in and solving the issue quickly, she was undermining the synergy of the group.

Much of Abby's work centered around being more self-aware and catching herself when she noticed her impatience. One tool she used to develop her self-awareness was a journal. This tool was discussed in Chapter One, when I referred to tracking food and workouts, but it can be used in other powerful ways. I have been journaling since my mother died when I was seven. No one ever suggested it to me, I simply gravitated toward that activity intuitively. There are many ways to journal, and I suggest that, if this is something you want to try, you just start writing. Your words do not need to make sense—that is not the point. Journal about your intentions, what you feel, how you acted, how you want to act, what you are grateful for, or what your goals are. I used to journal only when I felt crummy; now I journal every night. My clients have their own ways of journaling that they have refined over time. While some may write in a formal journal, others type their reflections on the computer or make notes in their phone. HSPs and introverts seem especially attracted to this method of self-awareness, but my extrovert clients are open-minded about it also.

The following case study focuses on a different aspect of emotional wellness but still demonstrates how the client was able to use journaling as part of his growth journey.

Case Study

Brent was the CEO of a pharmaceutical company, and he used his journal in an incredibly unique way to address impostor syndrome. This is a psychological pattern of doubting yourself and feeling like a fraud. We worked together to identify his specific impostor syndrome feelings, and, in his journal, he named them as if they were actual people. For example, he labeled self-doubt Doubtful Debbie, berating himself became known as Berating Betty, agonizing over the smallest mistakes was named Agonizing Andy, feelings of being a fraud were labeled Fraudulent Freddy. Whenever he felt overcome by those feelings, he welcomed them by name and had an internal conversation with them. This technique seemed to take the power away from the impostor syndrome, allowing Brent to feel more assertive, have more influence as a leader, and set a better example in the workplace.

Besides journaling, there are many other ways to explore and improve your emotional wellness. Each person must choose the method that works best for them, or experiment to find that out.

Another way to become more in touch with your emotions is through meditation. There are many forms of meditation, and I highly encourage you to explore some of them. I now meditate both in the morning and at night. In addition to being incredibly soothing, my meditative practices also provide me with remarkable insights—which seem to come later, rather than during meditation. My morning practice involves visualization, breathwork, and Kundalini meditation, while my evening practice is mindfulness meditation, journaling, and writing a gratitude list.

Another powerful way to grow your emotional wellness is to get outdoors. Being in nature has always helped me to become more in touch with myself. My trauma did an exceptionally good job at keeping me disconnected from myself, and I have seen it have the same impact on my clients too. When someone in the workplace is faced with microtrauma, like a bullying or controlling boss, a hostile work environment, or other dehumanizing situations, they become disconnected. They lose sight of who they are, their vision, and their passion. Trauma and stress are powerful, and it takes a deliberate, proactive, concerted effort to build resilience. Being in nature is a grounding method that puts you back in touch with yourself and your body. Some research even shows that walking barefoot in dirt, grass, or sand is incredibly grounding. Part of my workout regimen is to either walk or hike for about forty-five minutes each day. I purposely do not wear headphones when I am in nature because then I am able to focus on the sounds of nature and the animals around me. This type of nature awareness also contributes to mindfulness and reconnecting to a sense of place, in addition to exercise.

Breathwork is another tool you can use in any place and at any time. Your breath grounds you and brings you back to the present moment, where you can pay attention to your emotions. Since my clients spend their days fighting fires, resolving issues, and trying to pivot, they have little time to process internal or external events. Their behaviors are subpar because they are reacting instead of responding. The ideal response is a well-thought-out, proactive, and timely one. But how can that happen when there is no time to think? The answer is to use your breath, because it is always with you and you have complete control over it. There are many ways to do breathwork, and it can be done in front of others without them even knowing what you are doing. The resources section of this book offers some helpful breathwork activities.

For me, exercise grounds me and helps me stay in touch with my body and my emotions. It calms me, helps me sleep better, and helps me focus. I spend about ninety minutes each day doing strength training.

Sound is also very healing (and revealing) and can work wonders to return your focus to your emotions. This can be in the form of soft music, chanting sounds, or various instruments. Some of my clients play soft music somewhere in their background environment during each day to help reduce their anxiety. I incorporate sound healing into my daily meditations, and I also work consistently with a professional sound healer.

Many of my clients tend to lose their personal power during stressful meetings or potentially negative interactions. They become passive and experience feelings of intimidation, fear, impostor syndrome, and anxiety.

Case Study

That is what was happening to Belinda during her meetings. To help her get her emotions under control, we practiced a particular grounding technique in our coaching sessions. Belinda put her feet flat on the floor while standing. She immediately felt more grounded, in control, and more assertive. If standing is not possible, then stay seated, put your hands on your thighs, and focus on your own physical body. When Belinda practiced this in an actual client meeting, she reported that she felt more in touch with herself and her emotions. This type of grounding is a reminder that you "live here" in your body, and it helps you stay present during stressful times.

Yoga is another activity that is incredibly centering and calming. This is something you can do in a group or on your own at home. I practice yoga for thirty minutes each day and, over time, it has benefited me in multiple ways. It eases my sore muscles from strength training, reduces my anxiety, grounds me in my body, and helps me practice patience.

These are only a few of the strategies that can help you stay grounded and in touch with your emotions. And many of them cross over into other dimensions of wellness. Each person must find what works for them and then become consistent with using that method. Developing your emotional wellness starts with being aware of your inner landscape. These methods will help you do just that. But awareness is only the first step, because as emotions and triggers come up, you then need to handle them in a productive way. That is where many people falter. You may be able to identify your emotions and the things that set you off, but if you stop there, you are still at a disadvantage.

My childhood trauma and workplace microtrauma caused many triggers for me. Once I learned to identify the triggers and the emotions surrounding those events, the next step for me was to learn to sit with them, and not push them down. That meant that I had to explore them, address them, and handle them in healthy ways. Due to my cPTSD, I at first used various types of therapy to help me with that. But then I learned other ways to help that did not always involve therapy. I now use many techniques for what I call self-healing, but that was only after decades of traditional therapy, and I still rely on therapy when necessary.

I learned to create a support system for myself as well as a success team, which we will discuss in upcoming chapters. I also began to study self-compassion and Nonviolent Communication (NVC), which gave me huge insights into how to better manage my emotions and be more empathetic about others' emotions. I now introduce the basics of NVC to my coaching clients, and they have had great success with that tool.

Summary

- Improving emotional wellness can be scary, especially when trauma has been experienced

- Leaders are more influential when they prevent their emotions from controlling their behavior

- Working on emotional wellness helps you manage your responses when under pressure

- Managing emotions makes it easier to defuse emotionally intense situations

- The best way to start is to be aware of your emotions, explore them, and put strategies in place to address potentially unhealthy behaviors

ACTION ITEMS

Before moving on to the next chapter, please complete the following exercises:

- Listen to this webinar about dysfunctional thinking patterns[4]
- Complete the emotional agility assessment[5]
- Choose one grounding technique from Chapter Three, practice it for a week, and journal about your results

---

4 "7 Behaviors That Put Entrepreneurs at Risk | SCORE." n.d. Www.score.org. https://www.score.org/event/7-behaviors-put-entrepreneurs-risk.

5 "Quiz | Emotional Agility." n.d. Susan David, PhD. https://www.susandavid.com/quiz.

Chapter 4

RELATIONSHIP WELLNESS

Leaders need to know how to foster personal and professional relationships. It is best to build these skills first in your personal life and then transfer that knowledge to your professional life. While it is still scary and difficult, there is less emotional risk involved when you take those first steps privately instead of in the workplace environment. Accordingly, I will address each area separately in this chapter.

Now, we are going to explore the fourth dimension of wellness, called relationship wellness. This dimension addresses interpersonal relationships and the importance of creating support systems, developing and enforcing healthy boundaries, communication, and conflict management. Part of this dimension also involves tolerance, trust, concern for others, fairness, and justice. None of these components were present in my life as a child. Therefore, my relationship-building skills were not strong as an adult in the workplace.

Relationships and Trust

There is much professional research about attachment theory, which describes how our early relationship experiences dictate the ways we form relationships as adults. If you do not have healthy relationships as a child, there is a high possibility that you will not have the skills to develop them as an adult. After the loss of my mother, I had to rely on other adults in my life to meet my needs for love, emotional support, safety, and attention. One situation after another proved to me that adults could not be trusted, especially the adults who lived in my own household. This mindset carried over into my early professional life as I interviewed for jobs, managed my team, and tried to get promoted.

Even before my father abused me, I learned not to trust him. I experienced firsthand his willingness to abandon me when I disclosed to him and my grandmother that my paternal grandfather touched me inappropriately. As I did so, I watched with confusion and shame as my father turned and left the room without saying a single word. I may have been eight or nine years old.

Then there was the time when I pulled rags out of the rag bag and pinned them all together with large safety pins to make clothes for myself. I then went to school in that makeshift outfit. Of course, the school sent me home and called my father. He punished me by sending me to bed with no dinner, all while telling me he loved me.

And there was also the time when a relative and I were in our early teens and my father found a full pack of cigarettes in that person's bedroom. I had to watch as my father forced that relative to eat each cigarette in the pack. The relative was only allowed to stop eating long enough to vomit in the bathroom, then continue until the pack was gone. Afterwards, I was told to clean up the bathroom.

The abuse continued well into my teens, when my father would come into my bedroom during the night to spank me, bare bottom, for something I did "wrong." On one such occasion, when I was fourteen years old, I awoke, finding myself fully exposed from the waist down and being spanked over his knee. To this day, out of habit, I still lock my bedroom door.

How do you form solid, trusting, and supportive relationships when you were never taught how or never saw healthy examples?

For most of my young adulthood, and throughout my first marriage, I did not form friendships. I preferred to keep to myself. That was my solution to the lack of trust I developed. But, as I embarked on single parenthood and started my career, I came to realize that relationships are critical. Humans are not designed to live in isolation. We are designed to be interdependent, to support one another, and to provide empathy, compassion, love, and patience. This is the case whether "we" are partners, families, neighbors, teams, companies, customers, or nations.

Interpersonal relationships are extremely difficult to navigate. I am still learning how to do it—how to build trust with others, and how to continually refine my process. I will share with you the process I have come to rely on. This is the same process I share with my clients. I will delve into how to transfer it from your personal life to your professional life.

Fostering Relationship Wellness in Your Personal Life

My process involves creating a system of multiple people (who preferably align with your values), knowing and communicating your expectations with them (also known as setting boundaries), enforcing those expectations, and managing conflict when it arises. Let us break down this process one component at a time.

Aligning with Shared Values

How often are you deliberate and strategic when deciding who will be part of your social circle? My guess is, not very often. But if you were deliberate in making these decisions, here is what that would look like. It involves first being clear on your own values and then aligning with people who have similar values, or at least being willing to accept those who are not as aligned. This means that when you do meet someone, you are selective about letting them into your circle, because you allow only people who will lift you up and support you. I want to point out that being selective has nothing to do with shunning others, being overly judgmental, or being discriminatory. Your goal is to surround yourself with people who are healthy for your mental well-being and who know and validate your worth.

But how do you know this until you let them into your circle and get to know them? The answer goes back to being deliberate. Think through what you already know about them from others, consider brief experiences you have had with them, or get to know them slowly. Some people subconsciously do this anyway, but often those of us who never had good role models need some practice with this. We must consciously teach and remind ourselves of these skills. This also brings up another question—who is already in your circle that should not be there? In short, once you are clear about your own expectations, you can evaluate whether your current friends are living up to them. This brings us to the next component of building strong relationships—establishing and vocalizing your expectations.

Knowing and Communicating Expectations

Knowing what makes you feel supported, uplifted, and valued is your reality check when broadening your social circle. Learning these skills will also help you tremendously in the workplace when you must set tough boundaries. Having expectations is about recognizing how you want to be treated, what it means to be supported, and what you need from a relationship. Boundaries will be different for each individual, and determining them will be more difficult for those of you who have suffered trauma. Trauma skews our perception about expectations and boundaries, making it hard to understand what we really need and how to ask for it. But there is much more to having expectations than just knowing what they are. To make actionable change, you must communicate those expectations. My clients really struggle with this, and we spend a lot of coaching sessions crafting conversations about how they can communicate their expectations, either at home or at work. We usually employ the Bottom Line Up Front (BLUF) technique or Nonviolent Communication (NVC) strategies which we will discuss in later chapters.

Take, for example, the shifting in expectations between myself and a (now former) friend named Leslie. Leslie and I knew each other for almost fifteen years and started spending more time together over the last two years of that timeframe. We went to movies together, got together for lunch, shared personal details about our lives, discussed our work, and talked on the phone. I began to realize that a theme was developing in all our conversations. Leslie did most of the talking, totally monopolizing the conversations, while I listened. Any time I turned the conversation to myself, she quickly found a way to turn it back to her. My expectation for this friendship was for her to display equal sharing and listening time, and to show true concern for what was going on in my life (knowing my expectations). I became really annoyed with her pattern of overtaking conversations and decided to bring it to her attention (setting the expectation). To my amazement, before I had a chance to share my expectations with her, in our next phone conversation, she apologized for always taking over the conversation and thanked me for being such a good listener. I was very relieved that I did not have to embark on my planned difficult discussion with her. Unfortunately, my relief did not last long, which brings me to the next step of this process.

Enforcing Expectations

Once you know your expectation and share it with someone, you also need to be prepared to enforce it with a consequence if the person does not honor it. Leslie continued with her annoying behavior, even after acknowledging it and apologizing for it during multiple later conversations. I finally let her know that we would not be having many more conversations if this kept up. I was crystal clear that I felt unheard, and that I had an expectation of mutuality in our conversations.

Even if my clients get to the point of knowing and communicating expectations to others, enforcing those expectations is extraordinarily painful for them. This involves quite a bit of assertiveness, and you must be willing to follow through or you lose integrity with yourself and others. Unfortunately, Leslie did not seem interested in changing her habit, so I ended our fifteen-year friendship.

There are times when you might not have the luxury of walking away from an annoying person or situation. In the workplace, you cannot choose to interact only with people who are kind and in alignment with your values. Regrettably, dysfunctional employees know this on some level and consciously or subconsciously leverage this knowledge to propagate workplace abuse. Even when that is the case, you still cannot abandon this process, because you will be abandoning yourself. This brings me to the final component of this process: managing conflict.

Managing Conflict

Relationship wellness will almost always involve managing conflict, and even those who have not been traumatized struggle with this skill. The bottom line is that most conflict should be managed with the goals of staying in integrity with yourself and preserving the relationship if possible, and with the following things in mind:

- Respect
- Fairness
- Empathy
- Compassion
- Asking open-ended questions
- Understanding the other person's values, wants, and needs
- Listening
- Psychological safety
- Boundaries
- Staying open to alternatives

Relationship wellness is hard work because it involves using many interpersonal skills to build trust. That is why it is best to practice it consistently in your personal life, and then use the same process in your professional life. Let's look at some examples of how this process has been used in the workplace. As a reminder, the four components are (1) aligning with shared values, (2) knowing and communicating expectations, (3) enforcing expectations, and (4) managing conflict.

Fostering Relationship Wellness in Your Professional Life

ALIGNING WITH SHARED VALUES

In the workplace, it is not always possible to pick and choose who to align with to get the work done. Yet you still must try to find common ground for the sake of the project, customer, or organization. In the following example, Jason not only tried to find alignment, but also took an additional step to forge a cross-functional relationship, which was an effective way for him to also manage the conflict with Kevin.

Case Study

My client Jason was having trouble working with a peer, Kevin, who was in the same division in the company. Kevin seemed defensive, condescending, and uncollaborative whenever Jason tried to engage with him. During coaching, we brainstormed how to resolve this, and Jason decided to have a conversation with Kevin to see if there was any common ground. It turned out that in Kevin's mind, Jason had not yet proven himself, since he was so new to the company, and Kevin felt threatened. This is not unusual and often resolves itself with time. Jason also learned that Kevin had a strong alliance with a coworker named Brent, who worked in a different functional area. Ironically, Jason and Brent had just been placed on a project together, so Jason made a special effort to forge a trusting relationship with Brent. This was an indirect, nonmanipulative way to enhance his relationship with Kevin. Brent was very vocal about the success of the project across both functional areas. In record time, Kevin's attitude toward Jason shifted because of Brent's endorsement.

KNOWING AND COMMUNICATING EXPECTATIONS

Sometimes you are not even aware of your own expectations, or you are aware but do not know how to communicate them. In another case study, Sarah recognizes that she needs to promote herself better and build relationships (knowing her expectations) to receive a promotion (communicating expectations).

Case Study

Sarah was a client who had been passed over twice for promotion. The only feedback she received was that during high-stakes calibration meetings, no one really knew much about her accomplishments. When she brought this information to coaching, we developed a plan to reverse this perception and build a business case for her promotion. We put together strong accomplishment statements, a list of ten top leaders in functional areas other than her own, and a cadence of informational interviews in which she could get to know all ten people. Sarah worked hard in coaching to learn how to articulate her accomplishments, weave them into her conversations, and promote herself and her team. She came to terms with the difference between bragging and self-promoting. The former is inappropriate; the latter is expected in the business world. While I see this dilemma with both male and female clients, it is particularly common with women. Over time, Sarah built strong relationships across the entire organization, shifted others' perceptions, and validated the case for her promotion, which she received in the next promotion cycle.

ENFORCING EXPECTATIONS

Sometimes expectations are known, communicated, and agreed upon by all parties, and then things change. It is common for this component to be negotiated so that it is still a win-win situation for all parties. Enforcing expectations does not always mean that someone must lose, but it does mean that all parties must be willing to communicate.

Case Study

Deborah was a highly skilled IT technician dedicated to one functional area as the support person. She wanted to differentiate herself by developing a cross-functional skill set so that she could assist in other functional areas if those areas were short-staffed, or someday move into a different functional area altogether. In coaching, we developed a plan for her to be cross-trained in the other functional areas. This meant that she would agree to take internal training, shadow her peers in other departments, and take on stretch assignments in those departments. Her manager loved the idea and allowed her to immediately set up informational interviews with the leaders of those areas, which then led to their agreement to Deborah's plan.

MANAGING CONFLICT

Sometimes when expectations are not being met and ultimatums have been issued, tension and conflict can arise. However, with hard work, the conflict can result in a positive outcome and growth can take place.

Jennifer was a senior director who struggled immensely when giving corporate presentations. Not only was she nervous, but she also could not connect with her audience. As a senior director in IT, part of her job was to convince internal business partners to begin using new products and upgrades designed by her team. She had been doing the same presentation for three years with minimal results. Her conversion rate was low, and it was impacting her team's metrics. Jennifer had gotten a lot of negative feedback from her superiors for not bringing on new internal customers. She received an ultimatum from her manager to improve within thirty days if she wanted to keep her job. In coaching, we worked on practical changes as well as deeper behavioral shifts. When delivering her next presentation, Jennifer was able to:

- Communicate with more poise and confidence
- Enhance verbal and nonverbal communication to project a more professional presence
- Improve the structure of her presentation to better communicate the product features
- Use email in a unique way to connect with her audience before the presentation
- Improve listening skills so that she could respond to questions more quickly
- Deploy post-presentation demos to enhance connection to her audience

Jennifer brilliantly executed a forty-five-minute presentation after only one month of honing these skills. She had a 70 percent conversion rate from an audience of one hundred! Not only did she build relationships with her audience, she was also able to repair the relationship with her manager.

Growth Takes Time

I will round out this chapter with one last personal example that I am not very proud of, but it exemplifies the poor relationship-building skills I had when I began my career in my early twenties. As a single parent, I applied for my first office job, which had great pay and benefits. I submitted my resume three times over the course of a year before finally being called for an interview. I was frustrated by the delay because I had really wanted the job and, in the meantime, I had settled for a position I didn't want. I went through the interview process and got the job. On my first day, I met with my new manager. She expressed her excitement about having me on board. I responded with the most horrendous statement imaginable! I said, "Thank you, I'm happy to be here, but I submitted my resume three times—what took you so long?" I cringe even now when I think of how I must have been perceived. While I am still not perfect in this dimension of wellness, I have certainly come a long way in building relationships.

Having a strong dimension of relationship wellness is critical in both your personal and professional life. Not only do you want to have a solid support system for yourself, but as a leader, you want to set a good example by also having a strong network of business relationships.

Summary

- A strong foundation of relationships can be built by being clear about your values, knowing and communicating your expectations, enforcing expectations, and managing any conflict that arises

- Being selective about your relationships does not mean being discriminatory

- Sometimes you must try your best to find alignment for the sake of others

- Enforcing expectations takes assertiveness, but that skill can be learned

ACTION ITEMS

Before moving on to the next chapter, please complete the following exercises:

- In your journal, list an expectation you have that you would like someone to honor

- Craft a sample sentence about how you would communicate that expectation

- Then, list possible consequences that you'd be willing to enforce if they don't honor your expectation

Chapter 5

SPIRITUAL WELLNESS

The fifth dimension of wellness, spiritual wellness, means different things to each person. Some might sum it up by simply calling it intuition, while others call it religion. Still, others refer to it as the higher power. I believe spirituality includes all these things and much more. Developing spiritual wellness can be done with consistent practice. By exploring this fifth dimension of the first pillar, you will gain a better understanding of what spiritual wellness means to you, ways to deepen it, and how to integrate those preferences into your professional life.

Why is it important to understand, develop, and integrate your spiritual wellness into your professional life? To advance in your career and lead successfully in the workplace, you must have a strong foundation that keeps you grounded and connected to yourself.

Many of my executive clients flounder when it comes to decision-making, struggle with ethical issues, or get caught up in moral conflicts—especially in toxic corporate environments. They get derailed, hesitate to act, contribute to conflict, or make subpar decisions. These situations eventually lead to coaching sessions that focus on their value system. However, it is my belief that a precursor to working on values is spiritual work. The topic of spirituality sometimes comes up in coaching and sometimes does not, depending on the direction the client wants to take. To me, spirituality is at the core of a person's value system, with that value system developing out of their spiritual beliefs. It is also my opinion that most people have a spiritual foundation even if they do not realize it. While that foundation may be underdeveloped, unrecognized, or a combination of beliefs and experiences—it exists.

Below are some examples of how my clients define spirituality for themselves. Does anything on this list resonate with you?

- Intuition that seems to guide your decisions and behavior
- A strong pull toward organized or traditional religion
- A feeling of connectedness to yourself and others
- An interest in ancient belief systems
- An inner knowing that certain decisions are right for you
- A sense of wisdom that comes from within yourself, yet feels a bit foreign
- A sense of compassion, empathy, and justice that causes you to feel responsible for others
- A continuous drive, motivation, or inspiration that moves you to action for no apparent reason
- The ability to experience total clarity and direction during massive chaos
- A feeling of inner peace, tranquility, or empowerment

For the sake of space, I will end the list here. I will discuss each example in more detail later in this chapter. As you look at the list, you may find that nothing there resonates with you, or that you do experience certain things on the list but only occasionally. Or you may experience just a few of them, but very strongly. Still again, you may be completely aware of them all, in addition to many more that are not on the list. Your ability to experience and recognize forms of spirituality will depend on how developed you are in this dimension of wellness. Developing this area, or your inner voice, helps you define your purpose and direction. This has a massive impact on how you lead in the workplace. Your strength and influence as a leader and the example you set will be based on how you cultivate this dimension of wellness.

There are many things that can fracture spiritual development, crush inspiration, and silence your inner voice. Things like trauma, workplace microtrauma, life transitions, or simply being in a fast-paced corporate environment are all culprits that can diminish your inner radiance. As a child, my inner voice was silenced by the abuse and neglect that I experienced. Fear took over. It became ingrained in me not to fight back. For instance, I never protested when I was only allowed to shower once a week as a teenage girl. I also didn't resist when I was told to withhold food from my pets.

These circumstances put you in survival mode and make it nearly impossible to develop spiritually. Toxic corporate culture encourages employees to disconnect from themselves and each other. They operate from a place of unbending logic, formality, rigidity, and compliance. But the result is loss of creativity and innovation, unproductive teams, groupthink, lack of enthusiasm, and unfulfilling careers. Leaders lose their direction and purpose, which exacerbates toxicity and discontent. That becomes the price we pay for not recognizing and honoring our deeper spiritual side. Let us explore the previous list in detail, with real-life examples, so that you can identify areas where you can foster more spiritual wellness. Make some notes about which ones resonate with you, and add to your list if you think of more. Later in this chapter, we will talk about how to deepen those areas with consistent practices.

Exploring Areas of Spirituality

Intuition that seems to guide your decisions and behavior. The decisions that come from intuition may show up as thoughts, feelings, images, bodily sensations, or dreams. It is extremely easy to discount intuition, because sometimes what it tells us does not seem logical. This requires trusting yourself and acting on what feels like inspiration or divine guidance. This is a new concept for many people, but with practice, patience, and awareness, it becomes easier.

My intuition served me well at a time when my daughter was ill. Most parents have some type of inner knowing when it comes to their children. When my oldest daughter was ten years old, she became extremely sick. The illness began as a cold, but soon the symptoms worsened. I suspected pneumonia but did not really know why I thought this, because I had no medical knowledge of the symptoms. A trip to the doctor offered a diagnosis of bronchitis, and she was given an antibiotic. But the symptoms worsened further and required a second trip to the doctor.

At that visit, I meekly mentioned the possibility of pneumonia to the doctor, but he said that the sound of her lungs did not "meet the criteria." We left his office with a different prescription. Her cough worsened, her energy level and appetite dropped, and she became increasingly pale. I scheduled a third appointment and, by this time, I could not shake the constant nagging feeling that this was pneumonia. At the third appointment, I insisted on a chest x-ray.

I was not surprised that my suspicions were correct; she had pneumonia. What did surprise me was that she had double pneumonia. Even the doctor was shocked and still insisted that her lungs sounded fine. The doctor would not have done the x-ray if not asked to.

When have you had a keen sense of intuition about an issue at work or in your personal life? When this happens, do you listen to and trust yourself, or do you default to the status quo? Your intuition is there for a reason, and you need to listen to it.

A strong pull toward organized or traditional religion. While I am no longer Catholic, I practiced Catholicism for decades. It was the primary spiritual practice that kept me anchored through the many struggles in my adult life. I found much solace in prayer, silent retreats, weekly mass, and religious gatherings. I raised my children Catholic, and we took part in all the sacraments and Catholic social activities. As a matter of fact, their godmother is the same Catholic nun who took the three of us under her wing during my first divorce. I have tremendous gratitude to her for reintroducing us to the Catholic church and helping me form a strong moral base as a young single parent. Many of my clients have a devout religious practice that they lean on when they are faced with ethical, moral, or otherwise challenging situations in the workplace. Their religion forms the basis of their values, ethics, and morals.

A feeling of connectedness to yourself and others. One of the reasons I am writing this book is because I believe we are all connected and that my actions, whether positive or negative, have a domino effect and a major impact on others—even though I may never know who or in what way. At the beginning of this book, I wrote that we all have a responsibility to heal ourselves. One of the reasons for this is this concept of interconnectedness. When I work to heal my own trauma and transform as a human being, I am simultaneously creating a ripple effect that helps others heal. It breaks the cycle, shifts behavior, and allows me to own my trauma, tell my story, and contribute to a healthier environment and workplace. That feeling of interconnectedness, taking on that overall responsibility, is rooted in spirituality. This has been a very recent realization for me, and I must admit that I am humbled by it. We all must do our small part to make a bigger impact, and that willingness is spirituality at the core.

An interest in ancient belief systems. There are many ancient religions, philosophies, and belief systems which all include practices that contribute to the growth of spiritual wellness. I have explored Hinduism, Tantra, Taoism, and am now a practicing Buddhist. Many of my clients embrace ancient philosophies as part of their spiritual wellness and, like organized religion, these belief systems form the foundation of their values, ethics, and morals.

An inner knowing that certain decisions are right for you. This is a form of intuition. My client, Kate, had an adamant opinion about her department's budget. There was an additional $500,000 left in the budget at year-end, and she recommended that it be held in reserve, while her leader pushed for it to be spent so that it could be tracked as an expense, giving the company a tax break. Kate held firm and reported in coaching that it was a "feeling" she had that she could not explain and which she could not logically validate. Then COVID-19 hit, and many companies, Kate's included, needed all the cash reserve they could get their hands on.

A sense of wisdom that comes from within yourself, yet feels a bit foreign. Some of my clients report that they have always known their calling and, amazingly, they are experts in their field with little to no formal education. They cannot explain it, but feel they are called to impart their wisdom to others for the sake of others' success, and they are exceedingly good at it. Whether their knowledge or wisdom is shared through training, teaching, consulting, counseling, or being in any number of industries or roles, they excel as if they are divinely guided. This is a form of spirituality that has no logical explanation but, nevertheless, is benefiting society in tremendous ways.

A sense of compassion, empathy, and justice that causes you to feel responsible for others. On the surface, it might appear that people who experience this are simply very kind. However, my clients who feel this sense of responsibility share in coaching that these feelings are more like a sense of duty to others. They feel that, if they did not act on their feelings, they would literally waste away. Susan was one of my clients who experienced such a massive responsibility for others that it was almost debilitating for her. We began to unpack this in coaching because she was never in agreement with her manager, and they were experiencing conflict. As we worked through this, we discovered that Susan felt she had a "calling" to see that others were treated justly. This played out in such a way that she saw her direct reports as the "underdogs" and leadership as the "bad guys." This unbalanced mindset caused her to constantly advocate for her direct reports, even when it was not necessary or appropriate. She had lost her objectivity because of her intense inner voice that called for justice. In coaching, Susan had the insight that, while this was a spiritual part of her, it would benefit her to learn to manage it in a more balanced way. She also realized that sometimes leaders are the "underdogs," and she needed to look at each situation separately and then decide how to direct her energy.

A continuous drive, motivation, or inspiration that moves you to action for no apparent reason. I have seen clients with an immense drive and inner inspiration. They have no logical explanation as to what drives them, just that they are doing what they feel needs to be done. What causes some political refugees to escape inhumane conditions and become successful? What causes an at-risk teen from an underprivileged community to make it through college and become a productive, successful adult? Yes, they have "reasons" for wanting to get out of their conditions, but why do they succeed while their peers do not? Could their motivation, drive, and inspiration be of a spiritual nature? Could they have a spiritual calling, and be simply unconsciously following their inner voice without realizing it? And what does that mean for those who do not make it? Does that mean they are not listening or paying attention to their inner voice? Or that perhaps it is underdeveloped due to their circumstances? I do not have the answers to these questions, but they are food for thought. Personally, I believe we all have a spiritual calling, and the more we work to develop our spiritual dimension, the more we will recognize what it is.

The ability to experience total clarity and direction during massive chaos. Joseph was a client who had the unique ability to be in the middle of chaos, yet stay completely calm, manage his emotions, give direction, and keep everyone else centered. He was known within his department as an expert with change management and corporate transition initiatives. Change management initiatives are historically grueling, complex, and long-term-stress-inducing. But Joseph thrived on these initiatives and was exceedingly successful, which was validated with excellent metrics and high retention. Joseph did not know where this skill came from, but he considered it a spiritual quality. As a matter of fact, we leveraged this spiritual quality to prepare him for a promotion to Vice President of Change Management Initiatives. Joseph received the promotion, and then we worked in coaching on how to deepen his gift. What special quality do you possess that seems to bring you success almost every time? Do you feel it is spiritually rooted?

A feeling of inner peace, tranquility, or empowerment. Many people strive for inner peace and, like everything else, it is a journey. I imagine this feeling is a bit like what a child might experience when they are raised in a safe and healthy environment. They have no concept of distrust, no fear of violence, no framework for shame and humiliation. I did not experience that type of tranquility as a child; I was hypervigilant, so I cannot relate. Being shamed and humiliated were common, not only for me, but also for other family members.

On one such occasion, a young family member did something "wrong" and was spanked by my father with their pants down as I was told to sit on the couch and watch. The family member tried desperately to cover their private parts, but to no avail.

I do experience tranquility now, at times, and I am consistently working on it through my daily spiritual practices. Achieving even a glimpse of tranquility is exceedingly difficult for trauma survivors or those dealing with toxic work environments. Our framework of the world is different. Trust in a higher power can be fleeting, the world can feel unsafe, and thinking of the future can sometimes feel like impending doom. But I can attest to the fact that, with consistent spiritual practices, you can strengthen this dimension of wellness. Let us look at some things that I and my clients do to grow in this area.

Ways to Deepen Your Spiritual Dimension of Wellness

It is critical to note that you can have a list of spiritual practices the length of your arm, but the number is not what matters. It is consistency that matters most, so pick one or pick twenty, but practice daily. I had to work up to the number of practices that I now include in my daily routine. Deepening your spiritual side really boils down to quieting the outer noise of your world so that you can "hear" what is going on inside of you. For some, this is scary, annoying, fruitless, or too time-consuming, but I can honestly tell you that it works. I have also seen it work for my clients who are frazzled, stressed, feeling empty, and lacking enthusiasm and direction in their work.

Once you quiet yourself with any of the practices listed below, you will find that the answers you seek may come to you automatically, you become more centered, and you will show up at work with more influence and presence. You can also use many of these techniques to keep you grounded at work when you are involved in conflict, difficult conversations, or stressful situations or when your attention wavers.

Specific Spiritual Practices

As you read through this list, pick a few things that you can start practicing today.

- Anchoring movement: Dancing, walking, consciously allowing your feet to come into contact with the floor or ground.

- Animals: Put yourself in a place where there are animals (your own pets, a friend's pets, the zoo, a wildlife refuge facility).

- Breathwork: 4-2-7 (breathe in for a count of four, hold for a count of two, breathe out for a count of seven). This is only one example, but there are many other types of breathwork that will slow you down.

- Choice list: Make a list of all the things that you have free choice over in your life (e.g., I choose to breathe, I choose to change my mind, I choose to laugh, I choose to say no to anyone).

- Color in a coloring book: Yes, color.

- Desire story: Write a fairy tale story for how you want your life to be in the future.

- Exercise in whatever way you choose.

- Eye gazing: This can be done with a partner or with yourself by looking into a mirror. Eye gaze for two minutes and pay attention to what comes up for you.

- Go to church or temple, or take online spiritual classes.

- Gratitude list: List all the things you are grateful for from that day.

- Hand on heart: Place your right hand on your heart and just breathe. Feeling your body sensations is calming and puts you back in touch with yourself.

- Healing hands: Rub your hands together to generate heat and then put them on any part of your body that feels pain or upset or needs attention/healing. You are using your own powerful energy to get more in touch with yourself.

- Be in nature.

- I want list: Make a list of anything and everything you want in life—no matter how silly it seems. If you want it, write it down—allow yourself to dream.

- Listen to music or podcasts: Live, recorded, from your phone, etc.

- Loving kindness: Send thoughts of kindness to anyone (even yourself).

- Lunch with a friend.

- Massage.

- Meditate: There are various forms of meditation. Pick one that resonates with you.

- Museum trip.

- Movies: Watch a good-natured comedy.

- Nap.

- Permission: Give yourself permission to release someone, something, some feeling, some task, etc.

- Relational awareness: Practice being aware of two things at the same time. For example, be aware of your left thumb and the conversation you are having at the same moment. This keeps you grounded in the present moment, which is critical for spiritual growth.

- Schedule vacation time.

- Trauma release exercises.[6]

- Unstructured day: Take a day off and do not schedule anything, just do what you want in the moment.

- Visual journaling: Draw your feelings, instead of journaling them. This is a great way to express your feelings if you do not like to journal.

- What do I need?: Write or draw what you need in this very moment (e.g., money, a hug, compassionate words, quiet time, a friend, a phone call, etc.).

The list is not exhaustive—what other things can you add to it?

How to Integrate Spiritual Wellness into Your Professional Life

The workplace can be filled with stress, conflict, microtrauma, and inconsistencies. But it does not have to be that way. You

---

[6] "New_home." n.d. Tension, Stress and Trauma Release: TRE®. https://traumaprevention.com/.

can influence that culture. By transforming yourself with these spiritual practices, you can also transform your external structures. Identifying and enacting your spiritual practices will lead to more clarity on your values, which you bring to the workplace every day. My client Rochelle used her work on this dimension of wellness in an incredibly unique way.

Case Study

Rochelle had ongoing conflict with Damian at work. They were peers, and she felt that Damian was rude, verbally abusive, and lacking in emotional intelligence. She tried everything she could think of to smooth the relationship, including reporting his behavior to Human Resources. Due to corporate politics and Damian's position, his behavior did not change. In coaching, as we brainstormed possible solutions, Rochelle landed on one of the best possible solutions for her battered soul. She used her spiritual practice of meditation to get clarity on the fact that she could not change him, he would not change himself, and she needed to keep her job for the time being. Given that conclusion, she then decided to use her spiritual practice of writing a desire story to prepare emotionally as well as possible before interacting with him. Then she would use additional spiritual practices to work internally on the situation and take care of herself emotionally after interacting with him.

For Rochelle, having spiritual practices gave her the clarity to problem-solve, a sense of control over how to prepare for an interaction with Damian, and a way to take care of herself after the interaction. Having a strong spiritual dimension of wellness will benefit you at work when you must stay grounded during tough conversations, make objective decisions, and advance your career.

Summary

- Spiritual wellness means different things to each person—be clear on your definition

- People experience spirituality in a variety of ways that might not seem spiritual

- To begin exploring your spiritual wellness, you need to make time for quiet reflection

- Consistency is the key when implementing spiritual practices

- Spiritual wellness is the foundation needed to fully develop values, ethics, and morals

- Spiritual practices can easily be implemented in your professional life for more clarity, balance, and insight

ACTION ITEMS

Before moving on to the next chapter, please complete the following exercises:

- Journal your thoughts about how spirituality shows up for you

- Write down how much time per day you can devote to spiritual practices

- From the list provided in this chapter, list the types of practices you will commit to doing daily (or add your own)

- What practices can you begin to use immediately at work? Keep track of what happens

Chapter 6

ENVIRONMENTAL WELLNESS

As we progress through the first pillar of transforming yourself, we will now learn more about the sixth dimension of wellness: environmental wellness. In a broad sense, environmental wellness is a focus on protecting resources and enhancing personal safety. You are shaped by the environment around you, and that has an impact on how you lead. This chapter will help you explore what environmental stewardship and personal safety mean to you, and how you can lead better by enhancing this dimension. I will address each of the two areas separately, and the distinction between environmental wellness in your personal life and at work.

Environmental Stewardship in Your Personal Life

Environmental stewardship relates to your philosophy and behavior around the natural resources that you consume, and things you can do to reduce your ecological footprint. In previous chapters, you learned about being present and mindful and the importance of staying informed and being an educated resource for your coworkers. That state of mind and desire to educate yourself is no different when it comes to caring for your environment. Do you realize when you are being wasteful? Do you declutter and donate on a regular basis? In what way do you conserve energy, food, clothing, and spending? Do you have a conservation plan so that you are doing your part to protect the environment, or are you not informed about those issues?

Healthy ecological behavior can show up in the workplace as well as in your personal life. It can reach a global level, where you take part in large initiatives that will make a macro impact, or it can show up at a micro level, within your home and community. As a leader in all these areas—workplace, home, and community—you have a responsibility to understand how your existence as a human has an ecological impact. Having a perspective regarding environmental wellness will help you lead with more empathy and humility.

Case Study

Trisha, a client of mine, was an executive vice president who felt scattered in her daily work life. Intuitively, she knew that she was not great at setting goals in either her personal or professional life and that was causing her to feel ungrounded and directionless. She wanted to focus our coaching on how to set goals in both areas of her life. I offered Trisha a goal-setting tool and worked with her on a goal-setting process.

Part of the process focused on defining environmental wellness and helping Trisha figure out what that meant for her. Through our discussions, she determined that she did want to be more responsible when it came to ecological stewardship. As part of her environmental wellness goals, she created a conservation plan in her personal life. One of her first actions was to stop ordering fast-food delivery because it came with disposable containers and plastic utensils. She also realized that, because she ordered so much fast food, the food in her refrigerator was spoiling and had to be thrown away. A second action she committed to was keeping up with the routine maintenance of her car. And yet a third action was to coordinate the running of errands so that she could save gas. These were just a few things Trisha did on a micro level within her personal life to be more responsible about reducing her ecological footprint. Keep reading to find out more about what she did in the workplace.

There are many more things that can be done in the home and community, like shopping with reusable bags, installing drapes that block out heat, and following recommendations from utility companies about when to wash clothes or use the dishwasher. On a macro level, you can get involved in any number of global groups that bring awareness to climate issues, sustainability topics, or environmental activism.

Personally, I try to educate myself and act on topics that bring attention to pesticides in food, chemicals in water, climate change, purchasing local food, gas conservation, recycling, and chemical-free cleaning products. Once a year, there is a program in most states called Prescription Take Back Day,[7] when you can turn in unused medication to the Drug Enforcement Administration (DEA) and have it disposed of safely, rather than flushing it down the toilet or throwing it in the trash. On a broader level, I am also involved in some domestic and international volunteer activities.

It is important to note here that you cannot do everything, champion every cause, or be an advocate for every issue. Our society has suffered massive environmental destruction that may never be fully repaired—at least not in my lifetime or the lifetime of most of you reading this book. But every little thing you do helps, even if you falter at times. You might not see your impact, but just know that you are making a difference. Plus, you are setting an example for those around you, developing empathy for our planet, and displaying humility—a highly valued leadership quality. Our resources will not last without people changing their behaviors. Many of us, including

---

7 "National Prescription Drug Take Back Day." n.d. Www.deadiversion.usdoj.gov. https://www.deadiversion.usdoj.gov/drug_disposal/takeback/.

myself, are privileged to have access to goods and services at will. But that is not the case elsewhere in the world. There are shortages everywhere. For various reasons, shortages became reality for many of us when COVID-19 hit. When food was rationed and I also had to stand in line for toilet paper twice at six in the morning, it felt like a surreal situation, and it made me cry. As with your personal life, you can also have an impact on conserving resources at work, and here is what that can look like.

Environmental Stewardship at Work

Companies of all sizes need to consume resources so that they can produce products and services. It is part of doing business and consumption cannot be avoided, but you can be more mindful and deliberate about how and what you consume. Think about your behavior at work and reflect on the following questions:

- How often do you use the printer when you do not need to?

- If you have a long commute to work, do you carpool or take public transportation?

- Do you have any influence over the lighting or energy consumption in your work area?

- How often do you authorize travel for yourself or your direct reports? We learned during COVID-19 that many things can be done remotely.

- Do you use your own mug for coffee or tea?

- What kind of relationship do you have with the facilities manager in your organization, so that you can understand their maintenance policies?

- When travel is necessary, can you influence policies about how company funds are spent (e.g., hotels, car rentals, restaurants)? Conserving resources also means saving money when you can.

- What is the company recycling policy for paper, plastic, electronics, and batteries?

- Can outdated technologies that companies provide be donated to certain organizations?[8]

- In what ways do you encourage your direct reports and peers to be environmentally responsible?

These are just a few examples of how environmental stewardship can be incorporated into the workplace. Many companies also have robust corporate social responsibility (CSR) initiatives, which I will briefly explain because it ties in with this chapter.

Corporate Social Responsibility

Corporate social responsibility, in my opinion, falls under the dimension of environmental wellness. It is the philosophy that making money should not be a company's only goal, and that they also have a duty to act in the best interest of their environment and of society as a whole. Corporate social responsibility is traditionally broken into four broad categories (which include many subcategories): environmental, philanthropic, ethical, and

---

[8] Johnson, Craig. 2021. "9 Ways to Donate Old Cell Phones." Clark Howard. February 5, 2021. https://clark.com/cell-phones/donate-old-cell-phones/.

economic responsibility. Many of my clients who are job-hunting often consider which companies have a CSR policy and will not take a job with those that do not. More and more pressure is being put on companies—even small businesses—to be ethically, financially, and environmentally responsible for the greater good of society.

Remember my client Trisha, who put a plan in place to be more ecologically responsible in her personal life? I also worked with her to implement a unique tool to build environmental thinking into her department's business strategy.

Case Study

During our coaching sessions, I introduced Trisha to the book *Green to Gold: How Smart Companies Use Environmental Strategy to Innovate, Create Value, and Build Competitive Advantage* by Andrew Winston and Daniel Esty.[9] The book focuses on an excellent process, called an Environmental Management System (EMS), that I use within my own company. Here is an overview of how Trisha developed her own EMS plan. The template is based on four areas: planning, objectives, actions, and programs. It guides a person through the thought process related to the operation of their department or company.

Trisha had to think through all the vendors, suppliers, material, staff, contractors, utilities, and even the purchasing process of her department (planning). She then set goals and measurements to reduce consumption or save costs in all those areas (objectives). Finally, she created various standards, processes, and procedures to support the objectives (programs). The programs she created

---

[9] Esty, Daniel C, and Andrew Spencer Winston. 2009. *Green to Gold: How Smart Companies Use Environmental Strategy to Innovate, Create Value, and Build a Competitive Advantage.* Hoboken, N.J.: Wiley.

involved the updating of protocols around purchasing, contracting with vendors, hiring staff, and maintaining company vehicles and technology. The EMS process also involved a communication plan. Then she socialized the entire document with her staff and scaled the process to other departments. You can sum this process up as equivalent to a business plan or a strategic plan, except it is specifically focused on environmental stewardship within a company. Now that we have addressed the portion of environmental wellness that covers protecting resources, let us delve into the portion related to enhancing personal safety.

Environmental Wellness and Personal Safety

Any place where your physical body is located is considered your physical environment. Anything that goes on in your physical environment can impact you mentally, physically, spiritually, and emotionally (personal safety). So it is critical that your physical environment be safe in all those ways, be a place that reduces fear and vulnerability, and be a place that contributes to your empowerment. That is your responsibility to yourself as an individual.

In addition, as a leader, you are responsible for the personal safety of your coworkers within the workplace. If you have not already, you need to take steps to strongly influence policies related to workplace violence, domestic violence, substance abuse, and other acts that put the safety of employees at risk. If you are not aware of the policies, then become aware of them. Workplace safety is not just the responsibility of Human Resources. It is everyone's responsibility.

The Corporate Alliance to End Partner Violence "found that 21 percent of full-time employed adults said they were victims of domestic violence and 74 percent of that group said they've been harassed at work." Yet 65 percent of companies don't have a formal workplace domestic violence prevention policy, according to research conducted by the Society for Human Resource Management. Only 20 percent offer training on domestic violence, the 2013 survey found.[10]

During my corporate career, I held domestic violence education seminars in many of the companies where I was employed. I also volunteered in domestic violence shelters as a speaker, mentor, and fitness trainer for the women who lived there. Additionally, I educated the public by speaking to the media about the topic of domestic violence and by sharing my story.

At the time of this writing, workplace violence is on the rise, and the outlook for the safety of employees is not good. As an HSP and someone with cPTSD, I am extremely sensitive to all types of potentially unsafe situations. This is the case even after decades of trauma work. I was hyper-alert to danger in the workplace, especially after being stalked there during my first divorce and after being bullied by two managers.

I coach many leaders who have not yet healed from personal trauma, and yet they face still more trauma and microtrauma from being in unsafe work situations daily. In the case study below, you will read about Jose, a political refugee who gained citizenship in the United States. He worked extraordinarily hard to make a living, work his way up in corporate America, and provide a safe home for his family.

---

10 "When Domestic Violence Comes to Work." n.d. Www.shrm.org. https://www.shrm.org/topics-tools/news/risk-management/domestic-violence-comes-to-work.

Case Study

Jose was a coaching client who came to his first session visibly distraught. He explained that he was having a situation with his manager and needed help with some better communication techniques. He wanted to work on "reducing his foreign accent" and "improving his English" so that his manager could understand him better when communicating. He explained that English was not his first language, and his manager felt that was a hindrance to his ability to follow instructions. Jose felt that he did follow instructions, but stated that his manager would change them and deny giving the original set of instructions. His manager was also withholding deadline information and then berating Jose if a deadline was missed. Jose was confused by this and, over time, his manager's behavior slowly chipped away at his self-confidence. Apparently, the manager would also mock his accent and would embarrass him in front of coworkers if he used an incorrect English word.

As we unpacked this in coaching, Jose realized this was not a problem with his performance, his communication style, or his accent. He was experiencing gaslighting and microaggressions from his manager, which made him feel embarrassed and unsafe and impacted his ability to navigate specific work situations. He promptly filed a complaint with Human Resources, and they took appropriate action.

Personal Safety Includes Psychological Safety

As a leader in the workplace, you are obligated to provide an environment of psychological safety for your direct reports and coworkers. Psychological safety is a shared belief by members of a team that they will not be punished, ridiculed, or rejected for speaking up. Coworkers should be able to openly address fears, questions, concerns, beliefs, and opinions in a safe environment. That is part of the personal safety component of environmental wellness.

Here are some ways to foster psychological safety on your team:

- Use active listening skills like nodding, eye contact, or asking follow-up questions
- Encourage respect, and respectful disagreements
- Set the example
- Admit your own mistakes
- Keep an open mind
- Provide training on psychological safety
- Share your personal experiences and encourage others to do the same

We have addressed the components of personal safety and your obligation as a leader to keep your coworkers physically and emotionally safe in the workplace. I am going to make a turn here and discuss ways you can create personal safety for people outside of work.

Providing Personal Safety to Others Outside of the Workplace

Empowering others contributes to their sense of safety and well-being within their environment. There are many people who are vulnerable because they experience a lack of skills in areas such as language, literacy, parenting, employment, finance, health, or driving. Lacking any type of skill can create disparity, set people up for more challenges accomplishing tasks, and cause them to feel unsafe and insecure. I felt that way initially as a single parent. I was a high school dropout with no work experience, I could not drive, and I was living below the poverty level. (I did not learn how to drive until I was twenty-two years old.) I can assure you that I felt vulnerable, and many people tried to take advantage of my situation.

What can you do to provide security, safety, and empowerment to vulnerable people within your environment? Volunteer work has always been important to me as a way to give back within my community and across the globe. For me, it is a part of environmental wellness that cannot be overlooked.

I started volunteering in my late twenties for my church and for domestic violence shelters. I have traveled to China to volunteer at Sias University, teaching leadership classes to young Chinese women. Today, I am certified as an English as a Second Language instructor and have taught ESL classes locally to immigrants. In the summers, I travel overseas to provide volunteer services to foreign business executives in conversational English programs. I am a trained volunteer for the International Rescue Committee and for Amnesty International. My daughters also volunteered when they were younger because I thought it was important to instill that message.

Again, you cannot do everything and champion every cause, but you can determine what is important to you, focus on it, and create time for it in your schedule. Is there an area in which you would like to volunteer? Even many companies, as part of their CSR initiatives, do a donation match or allow their employees to volunteer on company time.

Environmental wellness is such an important part of your personal and leadership journey. We are all connected, so even your small actions can have a huge impact on the environment and its people, whether it be globally, at a community level, or at work.

Summary

- Environmental wellness includes protecting resources and enhancing personal safety

- You can reduce your ecological footprint in many ways in your personal life and at work

- Many companies have a CSR policy in place

- An EMS is a way to incorporate environmental thinking into business strategy

- Personal safety involves safety at work and in your personal environment

- Safety at work includes being safe from domestic and workplace violence, at a minimum

- Psychological safety is part of workplace safety

- You can create safety for others and reduce disparities outside of work by volunteering

ACTION ITEMS

Before moving on to the next chapter, please complete the following exercises:

- In your journal, write down what you consider your macro and micro environment

- Then write down ways you can influence the environment around you

- Review the EMS process and, if it resonates with you, create one for your work area

Chapter 7

OCCUPATIONAL WELLNESS

Too many leaders start their careers without a clear idea of their true passion, skills, and strengths. I entered the business world for the sheer purpose of making money to survive as a single parent. And because I did not clearly know my true calling, I made many mistakes in the workplace. This chapter about occupational wellness will help you explore your career interests and professional skill gaps that need to be addressed along the way. In addition, you will discover how to position yourself for promotions. You will also be introduced to an individual development plan as a tool to keep you focused on your next career steps. An effective leader has vocational satisfaction and a good balance of work and leisure.

Some people are fortunate enough to know their career direction from an early age. For example, my oldest daughter was only twelve when she decided to be an elementary school teacher. She was influenced by her fourth-grade teacher and planned all her high school courses, college coursework, and volunteer work around that career path. She has spent years teaching at-risk kids in schools in Detroit and Chicago. Like my daughter, some of my clients have been very deliberate about their career choices. Meanwhile, others accidentally fell into fulfilling careers. And others are still struggling to figure out their passion.

Leading from All Levels

One thing most of my clients have in common is that they want to make a difference in the workplace by rising to top-level positions. They just do not know how to, because there are barriers like office politics, bosses who block their promotions, and budget constraints that put promotions on hold. The other common challenge is that they have undeveloped skill sets that they do not know how to cultivate. It is important to note that you do not need to be in the C-suite to make a difference. Anyone can lead and make an impact, no matter what role they occupy. This point is well illustrated in Robin Sharma's book *The Leader Who Had No Title*.[11]

There is also the mistaken notion that, if you do get to the C-suite, people will automatically listen to you and seamlessly implement your vision. But that depends on several things—how passionate you are about the role, if you have the right skill sets, if you leverage your strengths, and if you have positioned yourself correctly to influence others. Let us work our way through these items one by one.

Exploring Your Career Passion

You must know your inner passion when it comes to your profession because work is where you spend most of your time until retirement. Your ability to make a difference in the workplace is directly related to your passion about the role. If you are not happy, you will make everyone else unhappy, you will lead inauthentically, and you will become a toxic boss. You

---

11 Sharma, Robin S. 2010. *The Leader Who Had No Title: An Inspiring Story about Working (and Living) at Your Absolute Best*. London: Simon & Schuster.

can explore your career passion with a career coach or career counselor, by taking assessments, or by simply reflecting on what brings you joy. Sometimes when people slow down enough to reflect on their career, they realize they need to make a huge shift. This was the case with Rodrigo, an executive director in a software development company.

Case Study

Rodrigo had worked his way up the corporate ladder quickly. He provided oversight to two teams, had built good relationships with other senior leaders, and had good work-life balance. But he had consistently felt discouraged, unhappy, and unfulfilled for the past two years. In coaching, we explored where this could be coming from. Eventually, he lit up when he shared with me that he loved to cook! In fact, his work-life balance was so good because he made sure to do as much cooking as possible when he wasn't working. He was happiest when he was home cooking for family. Almost immediately after sharing this, he had a light bulb go off in his head. Rodrigo shared that, as a young child, he had had a secret fantasy of being a chef in his own restaurant. I asked him to expand more on what that would look like to him, and he began crafting an entirely new career for himself. He also realized that, due to his successful corporate career, he had the finances to invest in a small restaurant. The rest of our coaching sessions pivoted to helping Rodrigo put together a business plan so that he could transition to a new career at the age of fifty-five.

Career shifts are not always this dramatic. Sometimes they are as simple as changing teams, roles, or departments. But you will not know unless you put deliberate thought and time into exploring what you are passionate about and how that relates to your career.

Also, your manager should have career conversations with you at regular intervals to help guide you. If that is not happening, then you need to take ownership and initiate those conversations.

Similarly, you should be having career conversations with your direct reports. You owe it to your team members to help them find their passion and develop it. An effective leader will do what they can to ensure their people are in roles that reflect their passion. Are you living out your passion in your current role? Are your direct reports?

Developing Your Skill Set for More Success

An undeveloped skill set could be another reason why you are unhappy in your job, lack confidence, or have been overlooked for a promotion. This does not mean the role is not a good fit for you. It could just mean that your skills need further development. In these situations, it is important to gather feedback, send out a 360-degree assessment, or do a personal assessment of your own to look for skill gaps. Hard and soft skills can be developed, but they must be identified first. Once you are aware of them, create a personal learning plan to improve, and let your manager know about it. That communication will go a long way to show your manager you are engaged and committed to proactively growing professionally.

Knowing Your Strengths

Strengths are different than skills—this is an important distinction. Strengths are qualities that come naturally to you with little to no effort. I have noticed a trend with my clients; they may have all the skills they need to do their job, but if they are not leveraging all their strengths, they will still be unhappy. Your job must be structured so that you can use your natural abilities. I highly recommend that you take a free strengths assessment after you finish this chapter. My client Melanie had a rude awakening when she took her strengths assessment—it made all the difference in her decision to stay with her firm instead of leave.

Case Study

Melanie worked in the document control division of a large law firm. She managed a highly productive team that handled developing and finalizing client contracts. Her division oversaw data, information, and documentation for the firm's largest clients. She loved her team and the firm but was interviewing for similar jobs with other firms. She knew that she wasn't happy, but she could not quite determine the reason. In coaching, Melanie took a strengths assessment and found that her top strength was relationship building. She loved people, helping them, and forming deep relationships with them. After further analysis, Melanie realized that she really wanted to be more client-facing. Those were the types of relationships she was most passionate about—orienting new clients to the legal team, helping them through the details of their paperwork, and making sure they stayed happy during their legal journey. When she told her manager about this, he quickly arranged for her to transition to that type of role. The new role was perfect for her given her strength of relationship building and her experience with documentation.

Can you imagine what it would have been like if Melanie had taken a similar job with another firm, without being clear on her strengths? She most likely would have ended up in a similar role, with limited opportunities to foster relationships. Thinking critically about her strengths saved her from potentially spending years trapped in the same cycle. Many people spend years going from job to job, never realizing that their unhappiness simply stems from not tapping into their strengths. How clear are you about your skill set and strengths?

Positioning Yourself to Influence

For leaders who have a deep passion to make a difference, it is natural to want to do so from top-level positions. Because, even though you can lead without a title, it can be easier to make a difference at the top. And for those who are passionate about their jobs, have the right skill set, and know how to leverage their strengths, C-suite roles make perfect sense. That brings us to the topic of influence. The definition of influence can be difficult to articulate. Almost all my clients want to work on influence as a goal in our coaching sessions. It can mean different things to different people, and in different corporate cultures. However, when my clients say that they want to make a difference, they mean that they want to be able to influence teams, peers, senior leaders, and clients. They want to create a better culture, higher-performing teams, and safer workplaces. They want a seat at the table, and they want their vision and ideas to be heard and acted upon. That is a heavy lift—and just how do you do it? How do you structure your own occupational wellness to be able to achieve this goal?

From my own corporate journey and experiences with clients, I have discovered that gaining and maintaining influence is a marathon, not a sprint. The skills of influence are a combination of soft skills that take years to develop. That is why you must start early in your career, be deliberate and reflective, get feedback, and seek support. But if you do this, then it is very possible to earn a place at the top and make a difference. One of the most powerful forms of support to help you get there, besides a coach, is a mentor. There is a difference between a coach and a mentor, and I always suggest that my clients work with both. A mentor is usually (but not always) someone internal to your company who knows the company culture, is familiar with the unwritten rules, and can help you navigate the complex personalities.

I never had a mentor in any area of my life, but I wish I had, especially in my career. It would have been much easier for me to steer clear of critical mistakes, recover quicker from faux pas, understand my strengths, and build my confidence. You can even have more than one mentor, and it is important for your direct reports to have one too. A formal mentoring program is ideal, but if your company does not have that, then start an informal one. If you truly want to build your ability to influence, just know that it takes a combination of soft skills and plenty of support.

Positioning Yourself for Promotions

For those who truly love their career and want to move up, it is important to be deliberate about positioning themselves for promotions. Some of my clients have the passion, the skill set, and the strengths but still get passed over. Has that happened to you? Why do you think that is? Earlier, I mentioned office politics, bosses who block promotions, and budget constraints that put promotions on hold. We will address these pain points a little later in this chapter, but, in the absence of that toxicity, why else are you passed over?

I work with clients daily to help them prepare for promotions, and there is a strategy to be followed. A promotion is not something that normally happens by accident. For some, yes, a promotion has fallen into their lap. However, that is not the norm. Most of my clients do not prepare, do not follow a strategy, and do not display confidence when they interview. They also do not have career conversations with their managers, so their managers do not know they want a promotion.

When I was in my twenties, I made a very embarrassing, potentially career-killing comment to my manager. I saw three announcements that week of coworkers receiving promotions. After the third one, instead of congratulating that person, I stormed into my boss's office, shut the door behind me and said, "Why is everyone around me getting promoted, except me?" She looked at me dumbfounded and paused for a moment of silence. Then, she calmly said, "I didn't know you wanted a promotion." That was most definitely a cringe-worthy moment that I regret to this day. So, assuming you have communicated to your manager that you would like a promotion, there is a strategy to follow.

Follow a Strategy to Prepare for Promotions

1. Create a snapshot of your ideal future

    Determine your three-to-five-year career trajectory, your compensation package, where you want to be, and what that looks like for you.

2. Analyze the job description

    Assuming you have done the planning from step 1, you must plan ahead for the exact job you want. When you find it, analyze the job description to look for any gaps in your skill set. If you find gaps, create a plan to close the gaps, whether that be with technical training, internal soft skills training, or stretch projects. I usually recommend that people plan at least one year in advance before applying for any promotion, so that they have time to close the identified gaps. I recommend that they create an individual development plan (IDP) to help close the gaps.

3. Update your resume with accomplishment statements

    Most people have a resume that looks like a list of tasks, is too wordy, and not visually appealing. You only have about ten seconds to grab a hiring manager's attention, so your resume needs to be powerful and concise. Accomplishment statements are bullet-pointed impact statements that start with a verb and tie into a metric. You need to use your resume to articulate your value, not list the tasks of your job. Many of my clients think that it is bragging to show their value, but it is actually healthy self-promotion.

4. Update your LinkedIn profile

    Once you update your resume, you then need to update your LinkedIn profile. These days, if you do not have a LinkedIn profile, you are doing yourself a great disservice. This and your resume are two very powerful branding tools.

5. Increase your visibility with networking or informational interviews

    This step should become part of your daily existence within your organization, whether you are looking for a promotion or not. You should always be building relationships, learning what you can do for people, expressing your value, and articulating your desire for a promotion (if that is the case).

Internal networking is a little different than informational interviews, but the concept is the same.

6. Prepare for the interview

   I spend many sessions with my clients preparing them for the interview with Behavioral Interview Questions (BIQ). Practicing BIQ also helps them to articulate their value beyond what is in the resume. It is critical that you have examples you can share that point to what you have accomplished and how you have handled certain situations.

7. Interview follow-up

   There is always post-interview protocol that should be followed, like thanking the interviewer and connecting on LinkedIn.

While this seems like a lot of preparation, once you have gone through these steps for the first time, the bulk of the work is done when you apply for another role in the future. At that point, it is just a matter of keeping things updated and going through step 2 each time. I find that my clients' confidence builds drastically as we work through each step. That confidence makes a big impact in the interview, as it did for my client Matt, who was approached by four of the country's top tech companies.

Case Study

Matt had been with a small tech company for eighteen months and was not happy. He did not have good benefits, and the role was too demanding on his work-life balance. He wanted something different but really could not imagine being hired by any of the large tech companies he wanted to work for. In coaching, we went through steps 1, 3, 4, and 5. As his confidence grew, he began applying to external positions, which allowed us to then go through steps 2, 6, and 7. He became more self-assured, more comfortable articulating his accomplishments, and more eager to interview. One day I received a message from Matt that said, "This has been a great week! I've now got interviews scheduled with recruiters at four of the top US tech companies. Even during the days when I considered myself at the top of my career, I was never being considered by this many prestigious employers!"

My clients are living proof that preparation builds confidence! Earlier I mentioned that your career trajectory might be impacted by office politics, bosses who block promotions, or budget constraints that put promotions on hold. Just how do you get ahead in toxic work environments?

Staying True to Yourself

It is hard to do the work of true leadership just to be undermined by those around you. My clients struggle with this all the time. They have learned that they need to keep forging ahead, doing what they feel is right. It is the cross that every leader must bear, to stay in integrity while the world around you is not. As was mentioned in the beginning of this chapter, a true leader does not need a title. Their behavior alone will influence others and make an impact. So, focus on building relationships, living your values, being honest, having a voice when you can, and treating others with respect and dignity. Keep doing your work regardless of what others do. That is the only way to keep your sanity in dysfunctional environments that hold you back. But patience goes a long way also, as in the case of budget constraints. When COVID-19 hit, I suddenly saw companies stop spending money and put all promotions on hold. That lasted for one year, but I kept preparing my clients for promotions—we leveraged the extra time. The pendulum swung back, and then promotions couldn't happen fast enough. Nothing stays the same forever, so be patient. Your door will open, you will make an impact. You will get to where you want to be in your career with patience, passion, and planning. If you are being treated unfairly, and all else fails, you may need to escalate the situation to Human Resources.

Summary

- Leading can be done at all levels.
- Explore your passions to gain clarity about your job role.
- Identify your strengths and develop your skill set.
- Being an influential leader is a marathon, not a sprint.
- Work with a mentor to help you navigate internal company dynamics.
- Stay true to yourself in toxic work environments.

ACTION ITEMS

Before moving on to the next chapter, please complete the following exercises:

- Find and complete a free strengths assessment
- Follow the strategy to prepare for promotions

Chapter 8

FINANCIAL WELLNESS

What is your process for financial planning, budgeting, and saving money? The eighth and final dimension of wellness in this first pillar of transforming yourself is financial wellness. This dimension can be loosely defined as the ability to budget, save for emergencies, eliminate debt, save for retirement, and be responsible about the way you spend money. In some ways, this even ties into Chapter Six, about environmental wellness and spending wisely. In this chapter, you will examine your current financial situation, set financial goals, and identify the financial experts who can help you achieve those goals. You will also think through your long-term retirement plan and ways to prepare for that.

Your ability to be financially responsible in your personal life directly impacts your ability as a leader in the workplace. Why is this the case? At some point in your leadership career, you will be responsible for a project, department, or organizational budget. This is an area where some of my clients struggle because they do not like details, dealing with numbers, administrative processes, or planning. Plus, many people do not get a strong financial education from their parents or schools, so the topic of money becomes scary in the workplace. While it is true that the higher on the corporate ladder you climb, the higher the chance that you will have administrative support, you are ultimately the one responsible for crunching and reporting the numbers. If you are competent with this skill in your personal life, you can easily transfer it to your professional life.

Case Study

Maurice's main coaching goal was to prepare himself for a promotion to executive director. During the year, we focused on Maurice's branding, executive presence, influence, building relationships, and many other areas of soft skill growth. We were still in the midst of this growth plan when an executive director position opened. Maurice applied and—to his surprise—he got the promotion.

Although this was great news, we then had to pivot to begin preparing Maurice for the transition, which included overseeing a large organizational budget. I stand by my statement that if you can budget well in your personal life, you can also do it well at work. In Maurice's case, he was a good planner, and he had built many relationships during the year. He knew who to gather information from, who to tap into with questions, what the budget parameters were, how to track spending, and how to keep costs under control. Once he learned the internal processes and deadlines, it was just a matter of staying proactive when it came to this responsibility.

Budgeting Equals Planning and Tracking

As a single parent, I learned quite early how to pinch pennies and make it from one paycheck to the next. It is a simple formula; you must have more money coming in than you have going out. If you do not, then you either find ways to make more money, or you cut your outgoing expenses. This formula applies whether you oversee a household, a small business, or a division within a large company. I have done all three and, I can tell you, it is the exact same process. While it does get more complicated with the use of credit cards and lines of credit, nothing about the process will work if you are not planning and tracking. I encourage you to research and utilize some of the great tools that are available for financial planning. For many years, my only tool was a clean sheet of paper each month that listed my incoming paychecks and my outgoing expenses.

Your incoming monthly amount is easy to determine. But you will need to spend time tracking every penny you spend to know what your current financial health is. Most people randomly spend money without thinking about it and do not realize how quickly that adds up. Suddenly they cannot pay the electric bill, but they do not know why. Now, coming from an environment where I lived below the poverty level, I fully understand that sometimes circumstances make it difficult to balance a budget. However, you still must do your part—that's where the planning comes in. Once you have your income and expenses listed, you'll notice a deficit and then problem-solve to fix it. Many times, there are creative solutions that you can implement at the micro level.

What are you currently doing to keep track of your income and expenses? It is important to note that planning your finances is more than just planning from paycheck to paycheck. What would it look like if you planned your income and expenses for one year in advance? Sure, things can change during the year, but it never hurts to have a loose plan that you can adjust each month. What if you are trying to get a new job or a promotion? Your financial plan should be driving the amount of income, or the raise, you are striving to achieve.

As a single parent, one of my goals was to buy a house. But when I ran the numbers, I had no idea how to do that, because I had nothing saved for a down payment. Again, that tracking process allowed me to see the deficit and then problem-solve. I researched programs for first-time, low-income home buyers and found a program that would subsidize my mortgage payments and my closing costs. I ran more numbers to determine what my payments would be and immediately knew that I would need to make more money at work to afford them, even though they were subsidized. It was another year of raises and overtime, but I finally closed on that house! Then, imagine my upset when I realized the house did not have a stove or refrigerator. Yes, as a young, first-time home buyer, I overlooked that part and did not discover it until moving day.

Emergencies and Debt

On that day, I was left horrified as to how I would deal with my newest problem of purchasing kitchen appliances. Until then, I had had no credit card, but I did have a good bill-paying history—thanks to planning and tracking my finances. Against my better judgment, I applied for a credit card, received it, and purchased used appliances. I say that it was against my better judgment because I was terrified of credit cards. However, I have since developed the philosophy that it is not the debt that matters as much as how you handle the debt. I tried to be responsible about it, so I planned for the credit card payments, worked more overtime, and had the card paid off ahead of schedule. None of that was ideal, but I saw having appliances as a priority. Plus, the new credit card helped to build my credit history.

Many financial planners will tell you that, in addition to your living expenses, you must also pay down your debt, and save for emergencies. There is a financial formula for how much you should have in an emergency savings account, and that is different for everyone. According to Bankrate.com,[12] only 40 percent of Americans can handle an unexpected $1,000 expense, such as a medical bill or car repair.

What are your short-, medium-, and long-term financial goals? Are you mindfully and deliberately planning ahead to meet your living expenses, pay down debt, and save for emergencies?

You will have unplanned expenses at work too, like needing to hire someone unexpectedly. Or there's a great job candidate who negotiates a higher salary than you planned for, and you need to adjust. Or your company needs to comply with new regulations. And of course, you need to think about emergencies—like the expenses most companies endured during COVID-19. Be prepared for certain revenue streams to stop. For instance, you may have a top client terminate their contract, which will reduce company revenue. The more skilled you are at planning, tracking, and having reserves, the quicker you can pivot during a work crisis. It always comes back to your goals and priorities as the driving factors to your ultimate financial planning and financial wellness. One of the biggest goals to plan for that will impact you personally and professionally is your retirement.

Peace of Mind for Retirement

Many people look forward to retirement, and many do not. The clients I work with have mixed feelings about their current careers ending. Some of my clients have been displaced, offered early retirement, hit retirement age, or decide to leave the corporate world to start their own business. About 20 percent of my clients are leaving the workplace for one of these reasons, and not all

---

[12] Bankrate.com, n.d. "More than 1 in 3 Americans Would Go Into Debt to Pay a $1,000 Emergency Expense." https://www.bankrate.com/pdfs/pr/20190116-january-fsi.pdf.

of them are financially ready. Some choose to continue working past retirement age because they have not saved enough. Others take an early retirement package and find another job elsewhere. Others have been downsized and cannot find another job—and have not saved enough to be in this position. Still others are financially ready, but choose to keep working because they do not want to be bored. The situations go from one end of the spectrum to the other, which is why early planning is critical. Your financial wellness and your peace of mind will be directly impacted if you neglect to plan for retirement.

The best-case scenario is to have a support system of trusted financial advisors by your side over the long term to help you with this planning. My clients who have the best success with their retirement planning have had accountants, financial coaches, bookkeepers, financial planners, investment and trading advisors, and attorneys guiding them along the way. What financial experts do you currently have by your side? How have you planned for your retirement thus far?

Having a Financial and Emotional Plan

Making sure you are financially ready to let go of your main source of income is a massive decision—and some people do not have a choice. Planning is critical, and if you have a spouse or partner, then you need to include them in those conversations. Again, your plan may shift over time, but a loose plan is better than no plan at all. There are many books about the financial planning side of retirement, written by authors like Robert Kiyosaki and Suze Orman, but not many about the emotional side. Here is where my clients struggle the most. Even if they are financially ready for the next step in their life, many do not know what the next step is. In Janice's case, she had a great financial plan but lacked an emotional plan.

Case Study

Janice had saved for retirement since she was twenty, looking forward to the day when she could finally retire, reduce her stress, recover from the burnout of a fast-paced corporate job, and play golf. At age sixty, she had been offered a voluntary buyout by her company. With her buyout package and her retirement savings, she could live comfortably for the rest of her life. This was the day she had planned for since she was twenty, but where was her excitement? She had invested so much in her career that she never developed any skills for a second career, or any hobbies besides golf. Nor had she planned to retire early. At this point in her life, she could not imagine herself simply playing golf every day. She had a decision to make—take the buyout, or turn it down? In coaching, we worked on what her next steps could look like, what some of her passions were, and what would give her joy and keep her intellectually stimulated. She decided to accept the buyout, take a part-time job, and get involved in some volunteer work.

Those who do not psychologically prepare for voluntary or involuntary retirement can risk depression, dementia, hypertension, and other medical problems. This was the case with Marcus, who was displaced after twenty years with his company.

Case Study

Marcus was a client whose company went out of business. He was sixty-three years old, had not interviewed in twenty years, and only had a high school education. He was not financially ready to stop working and, even worse, he became severely depressed because he could not seem to find work. With no college education, no interview skills, and no professional brand to help him stand out, the situation did not look good.

In coaching, we worked on ways to identify and transfer his skills to other jobs and even to other professions and industries. But part of this work was about taking a step back to look at the bigger picture and figure out what his values, interests, and goals were for the rest of his life. By creating that plan, Marcus realized there were indeed other ways he could be of value in the workplace. Once he was clear on that, we were able to structure his resume and online profiles to reflect his strengths in the best light, help him with networking techniques, and role-play interview questions to improve his confidence. Marcus did find another job, and while it was not quite the salary he wanted, it offered educational reimbursement. Part of his emotional plan that we created in coaching was to pursue a degree. So, for Marcus, this job was the means to an end—a way to get the education he never had and to possibly take on a better role going forward.

The very life-altering change of retirement that many look forward to can end up being devastating once the day has arrived. But a solid emotional plan can make all the difference, like it did for my client Ralph.

Case Study

Ralph worked with his financial support team for decades preparing for retirement, had many conversations with his wife, and knew that his end goal after retirement was to do freelance consulting. Once he finally retired, he was able to seamlessly transition from his full-time job to running his small business. There was immediate demand for his services because he had spent time fostering those relationships on the side. Ralph was financially and emotionally satisfied due to the planning he did prior to retirement.

For some people, it is not enough to have a financial and emotional plan for themselves. They choose to also weave financial wellness into their interactions with customers at work. Just how does something like that take place?

Giving Value to Customers

The workplace is a complex system of relationships, communication, employees, customers, clients, leadership, services, and products. As a matter of fact, it is so complex that it is ripe for dysfunction. Many internal and external customers do not get the true value they deserve due to that dysfunction. The mindful leader goes above and beyond to show value to customers by helping them choose the service that works best for them, even if it is not the most expensive. These leaders will help the customer spend their money wisely by giving sound advice. They are proactive in identifying and mitigating risks and offsetting crises, so that the customer does not spend money unnecessarily. Leaders who are mindful about financial wellness in the workplace will mentor their team to follow suit, teach the team how to reduce expenses, and coach them to add value to the customer experience. That is how financial wellness is brought into the workplace.

Given all that you have just read in this chapter, there is one last critical point that I purposely saved until the end. I want it to be the final thought on your mind as we finish up this first pillar of transforming yourself and move into the second pillar of transforming your organization. All the planning, tracking, and implementing in the world will do no good to develop your dimension of financial wellness unless you address your belief system about money.

Negative Beliefs about Money

As you will learn in the next chapter about values, we are all conditioned by our upbringing. Along with that comes our belief systems—and those can be conscious and subconscious. We form our beliefs about money from what we have been told, what we have experienced, and what we have seen others experience. If those things are negative, it will impact our relationship to money, the ability to earn it, save it, spend it, or respect it. I grew up seeing my family struggle financially after my mother died. She had been the main breadwinner in the family, and after she died our financial security was threatened.

As I got older, my belief system revolved around thoughts that money is hard to get, you must work extremely hard for it, there is never enough, no one ever has enough money, and that you must suffer to get it. I had a lack-mentality when it came to money. I have had to recognize those beliefs and work to overcome them. Many of us never received a proper education about money while we were growing up. Once you begin to educate yourself about money, you will find that it is not that scary. Money can be a powerful tool to help you accomplish your goals if you learn to reverse your negative beliefs about it. What is your belief system around money? There will be further work in the next chapter on values in general. One small thing you can start doing right now is to treat your paper money with respect by keeping it neatly organized in your wallet and facing in the same direction. Give it a try and see what happens!

Summary

- At some point in your leadership career, you will be responsible for a budget
- Budgeting equals planning and tracking
- Income must be higher than expenses to avoid a budget deficit
- The budgeting process is the same in the workplace as in your personal life
- You must save for emergencies and be responsible about paying debt
- Planning for retirement will impact you personally and professionally
- You must have a financial and emotional plan for retirement
- You can bring financial wellness into the workplace
- Your relationship with money is directly impacted by your money belief system

ACTION ITEM

Before moving on to the next chapter, please complete the following exercise:

- Begin using a financial planning tool to create and track your budget

PILLAR TWO

IMPACT YOUR ORGANIZATION WITH INTEGRITY AND INFLUENCE

Pillar Two

INTRODUCTION

Pillar One focused on transforming yourself as an individual. By first enhancing your skill sets and mental approach, you will be equipped to influence others and make a difference in the workplace. Now that you have the tools to build up your own skills and confidence, you can implement them in your organization. Pillar Two includes seven chapters that will guide you through critical processes necessary to impact your organization and influence corporate culture. The chapters in this pillar will help you discover and align with your values, mission, and personal brand. You will then be shown how to use that brand to assert yourself in leading organizational change, developing others who can lead change, navigating corporate roadblocks, and communicating corporate vision down to the team level. You will emerge from this pillar with the skills to encourage cross-functional collaboration, build better relationships at the senior level, and communicate in a way that will reduce conflict and encourage healthy conversations and innovation.

Do you want to be a leader who can impact the organization at the highest level, influence other top leaders, and take part in conversations that structure corporate policies and behavior from the top down? If so, then delve into these chapters to uncover ways to do just that.

As I moved into the corporate world, I wanted to make a difference and use my influence to guide and empower others—clients, business partners, direct reports, and peers. The solutions I sought to make these things happen eluded me because the system was so broken, mismanaged, and filled with microtraumas.

I loved the thought of working in a world of teams, projects, deliverables, and seeing the outcome of my contributions! Even more exciting was my expectation of celebrating my team's accomplishments, moving on to the next awesome goal, and working on multiple goals simultaneously. But often it didn't happen the way I imagined, and it left me feeling unfulfilled. For decades, I was frustrated and burned-out from unrealistic deadlines, stringent metrics, and poor leadership.

Two Groups— Which One Are You?

It has been my experience that there are two groups of leaders in the corporate world:

1. Those who show up only for the paycheck, mismanage their team, and show no desire to really excel.

2. Those who truly want to lead, make a difference, and have a powerful impact on everyone in their path.

TWO GROUPS—WHICH ONE ARE YOU A PART OF?

Unfortunately, those in the first group are common in workplaces across the world, and their apathy shows in their words, actions, and outcomes. Their negative influence spreads like a virus. Those in the second group aim high, set a good example, and strive to be authentic leaders.

Now is your time to decide which group you belong to! If you are in the first group, now is the time to make a change. If you are in the second group, now is the time to find out how to lead in a more powerful way. I was always in the second group, but it was frustrating not knowing what steps to take to make an impact and not having a mentor or coach to guide me. This is the same thing my clients struggle with, but they also struggle with shifting their mindset, reversing old behaviors, and truly believing that they can excel in a dysfunctional corporate world. That takes a lot of courage!

Behavioral Change in Humans

The transtheoretical change model was developed by researching behavioral change in human beings. The research posits that there are various stages of change that a person goes through when they are shifting behavior. If you look at the graphic below, you are already beyond precontemplation and contemplation because you are reading this book. As you progress through the chapters in this pillar, ask yourself some questions. Why is it that you want to change your behavior? What are the negative consequences you will experience if you don't shift your mindset and act?

I want you to really reflect on these questions and even jot down some of your insights in your journal. This book is designed to set you up for success so that you continuously move forward with new skills, and without relapsing.

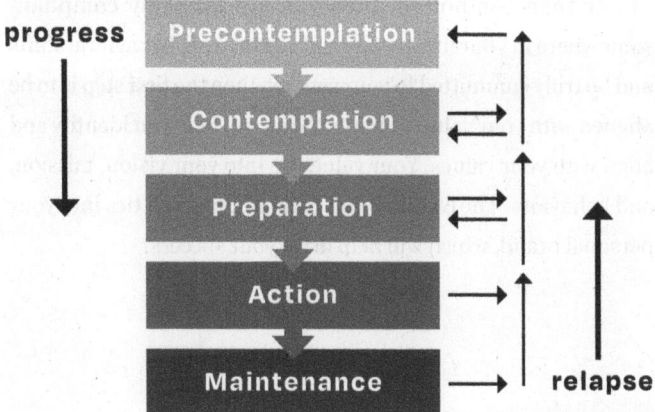

My background in psychology, coupled with decades of experience, has taught me that everyone has the ability to change successfully. This is true even when they are faced with seemingly insurmountable circumstances, like being surrounded by dysfunctional behavior or being engulfed in a toxic environment. You need to believe that change is possible! Even if you have tried hard in the past and got nowhere, this time is different. You will be leveraging tools, techniques, and strategies from this book that will meet you at any stage of your own process.

Change Is Easier When You Are Aligned with Your Values

Before diving into Chapter Nine, I wanted to address an important concept. Everything that comes into your life reflects your own action or inaction. If you cannot close a sale, you are most likely attracting clients who cannot connect or who are not aligned with your values. This probably means you are not aligned with your values. You may not know how to be—but it's your responsibility to learn. If your direct reports follow you because they are compliant rather than committed, then you are probably compliant somewhere in your life. If you want to make big behavioral shifts and be truly committed to your actions, then the first step is to be aligned with your values. Chapter Nine will help you identify and align with your values. Your values tie into your vision, mission, and behaviors. The combination of these things all ties into your personal brand, which will help drive your success!

Chapter 9

BEING ALIGNED WITH YOUR VALUES

Many leaders are confused about who they are and what they stand for, so it is not surprising that they cannot influence individuals at the micro level, much less at the macro level, of their organization. Do you want others to know who you are and what you stand for in your organization? Then you need to explore your personal and work values. If your role or the culture of your company does not align with your values, you are most likely in the wrong place. Here are some questions to ask yourself about your personal values.

Exploring Your Personal Values

Spend some time reflecting on these questions and jot your responses down in a journal. You may find that your values are different now than when you were younger.

- What values did I learn from my parents while growing up?
- What are some talents that I had when I was a child?
- What talents and strengths come naturally to me now?
- What are some activities that I loved doing as a child?
- What values do I have now, and how do they impact my decisions?
- What do I spend my money on?

- How do I spend my time when I'm not working?
- Is there anything I want to do with my free time that I am currently not doing?
- What values do I want to have, and what would my legacy be?
- How am I influenced by the values of others?
- What values *must* I live by to feel integrity?

Exploring Your Work Values

Work values can look a bit different than personal values, although ideally the two should be aligned. Work values are things like autonomy, money, developing others, authority, or making a difference. I have found that, if my clients are not fully committed at work and they are not getting their needs met, it is because their values are not aligned with the company. How can you lead effectively or make a difference at work if your needs are not being met?

If you are aligned with your values, and your values are aligned with those of your company, then people will trust you, want to follow you, and want to help you. In other words, they will acknowledge your credibility and buy in to your message. People will follow you because they are committing—not complying! And it is much easier to resolve business problems, increase sales, and decrease attrition with a committed team. This is true no matter what title you hold, because it is your outlook and attitude that draws people in.

My biggest hurdle when I was in the corporate world was aligning my values with the values of my organization. Unfortunately, it took decades for me to figure out how to do that. When you are in alignment, you have a natural spark, motivation, and desire to succeed in your role and within your organization. You truly *believe* in the work you are doing. Accomplishments seem to just flow one after another. But without that alignment, everything is an uphill battle. My client Julie experienced that uphill battle while working in a fast-paced public relations company.

Case Study

Julie valued work-life balance because she had three children and a husband with a chronic illness. Even though she loved her work in the public relations industry, her job was demanding, and she consistently worked over fifty hours a week. She routinely felt pulled in two different directions. She felt guilty, tired, and like she was not giving her best at her job or with her family. In coaching, Julie took the personal values assessment and the work values assessment. She could see for herself how out of alignment she was and that she was not being true to herself. This realization helped Julie make some important changes in her life so that she could be in alignment with her values. She was transparent with her manager about her challenges and was able to negotiate a reduced schedule that involved working from home two days a week.

In Julie's case, it was a struggle between her own values and the fast-paced company culture in which she worked. On the other hand, my client Chen was out of alignment because he was practicing values that were not his own. Instead, they belonged to his parents.

Case Study

Chen was a Chinese American man in his late fifties who, like Julie, worked fifty-plus hours a week. He was always the talk of the office because no one else there worked that much. His direct reports often felt guilty because Chen worked long hours, and they always went home at five o'clock. Chen began receiving feedback from his boss to "back off" and stop staying so late because he was setting a poor example for others. We began to unpack this in coaching by discussing values. After completing the two values exercises, Chen realized that growing up in the Chinese culture had molded his work ethic. He had learned from his parents that, like them, he needed to work long hours. He grasped that work and getting ahead in your career were priorities. He knew no other way, nor had he ever been taught a different perspective. This was a difficult shift for Chen, but he knew that his parents' values were not his own and that it was time to adopt new ones.

Values are the critical fabric that makes up the unique leader that you are. Authentic leaders are those who know their values, live by them, and stand by them no matter what. Values are your North Star, creating consistency in your life and helping you stay grounded when things get rocky.

Our values are shaped at an early age by our caregivers. In my case, my values and belief system were skewed by my childhood trauma. I entered the work world with no solid foundation or direction and was often defensive toward my bosses, angry at coworkers, and inclined to feel that my peers were out to get me. These reactions were the product of growing up in an environment of blame, shame, judgment, fear, and intimidation. My behavior at work was made worse by the frequent microtraumas I experienced there, like the time when I reminded one of my superiors about a promised deliverable from him that was beyond the due date. He suddenly started cursing at me at the top of his lungs and said that he was much too busy to remember menial things like that, and if I mentioned it to him again, I would end up "being a victim." I felt threatened by this statement and feared being fired. All these things were triggers that resulted in my inability to communicate properly, develop healthy work relationships, perform at my best, and set career goals. I needed not only a healthy set of values but a vision and mission for my life and career.

Vision, Mission, and Behaviors

After I left several jobs due to misalignment with company values, unhappiness, and lack of enthusiasm, I sought out a career counselor. I told her that I needed help finding a job or career where I did not have to interact with anyone. I thought I wanted something I could do that would not require any communication, conflict, or condescending authority figures. She administered an assessment that helped determine my values, vision, and mission. We met to debrief the assessment together. The results were shocking! She turned to me and said, "I don't think your true path is to be isolated with no interaction, or to sit tucked away by yourself. Your results show that you have tremendous empathy, high intellect and emotional intelligence, sincere passion for others, and a desire to make a difference." She went on to say that my results were pointing me in the direction of a "helping profession."

I was stunned, because I disliked most of the people I worked with, was terrified of conflict, and could not interact properly. In addition, I was never diplomatic and simply did not know how to "be" in the world. Everything overwhelmed me, scared me, and pretty much brought me to tears. How could I help others when I felt so debilitated? Nevertheless, seeking advice from that career counselor was a turning point for me. I began to get clear on my vision and mission. That internal work was the catalyst that, eventually, helped me identify my triggers and curb my unhealthy reactions and behaviors.

What Is a Vision?

There is often confusion about the difference between a vision and a mission. I will share my personal definition here. However, through this work, you might come up with your own. Your vision is the big picture of what you want to accomplish in the world, in both your personal and professional life. It articulates who you want to be, what you want to be known for, and the set of experiences and accomplishments you aim for. Your vision gives you a framework that helps define and evaluate your mission and goals.

I took the advice of that career counselor and tried to become clearer on my values, guiding purpose in life, and vision for my future. I asked myself the following key questions, which you can ask yourself too:

- What do I want to accomplish in life?
- If I look forward ten years, what do I hope to have accomplished?
- Why do I do what I do?
- Why am I in the role I am in at work?
- What do I want people to say about me at the end of my life?

What Is a Mission?

Once you have a deep understanding of your vision, you can then craft your mission. Your mission is the framework for how you will accomplish your vision. The mission answers a different set of key questions:

- What am I doing?
- Who am I doing it for?
- Why am I doing it?
- How do I do it?

A mission could be a full paragraph answering these questions. Answering the "Why am I doing it?" question might incorporate parts of your vision or purpose. But the bottom line is that your mission will go more into the details of how you will achieve your vision. I usually have my clients create this paragraph and then go one step further to create one succinct sentence that sums it all up. This is deep work in coaching, and it could take some time. But my clients emerge with a new sense of direction and purpose.

Behaviors

Your behaviors are dictated by your values, vision, and mission. If you cannot define these clearly, then it is difficult to be authentic, stand up for yourself, and lead well in the workplace. You will also find that your company has its own values, vision, and mission. As a leader, the sooner you go through your own personal process, the better you will be at aligning your behaviors with the expectations of your company. Misalignment in leaders shows up in their decisions, communication, assertiveness, executive presence, and overall confidence. However, being in alignment helps you to establish your personal brand. You can then weave your personal brand into all your work interactions.

What Is Personal Branding?

Personal branding is the authentic persona that you display to others in and out of the workplace. It is the entire package, that includes your authentic self, personal style, and leadership style, that is reflected in all you do. It is not only displaying that persona, but also developing a strategy of visibility to make sure others are crystal clear on that persona. Once my clients are clear on their values, vision, and mission, we then work on personal branding. I start each of my clients out by asking them three questions, and then we dive deeper into each one. The goal is to close the gap between steps 1 and 2 and arrive at step 3—an authentic depiction of you as a person and leader.

1. How do others see you?
2. How do you see yourself?
3. How do you *want* others to see you?

After my clients have reflected on these questions, we then create a plan for how they can portray their brand in all they do. This plan includes not only being more visible in their organization, but also incorporating their brand into their resume, LinkedIn profile, and interactions at work. The term "personal brand" has become somewhat of an ambiguous buzzword, causing many people to not fully understand what a brand can do for them. Knowing and portraying your brand can help you get hired quicker, build relationships, get a promotion, and be sought out by people who need your skill set. The goal is to walk your talk and show your authenticity. Do you want to be heard, be influential, and set a good example at work? Then get in alignment with your values, vision, mission, behaviors, and personal brand.

Summary

- Align with your values to shift your behavior
- Work and personal values are different

- Your vision is the big picture of what you want to accomplish in life

- Your mission is how to accomplish your vision

- Behaviors are dictated by your vision and mission

- Personal branding is the alignment of how you see yourself, how others see you, and how you want others to see you

ACTION ITEM

Before moving on to the next chapter, please complete the following exercise:

- In your journal, answer the questions in the above sections

Chapter 10

INFLUENCING ORGANIZATIONAL BEHAVIOR AND COMPANY CULTURE

What is meant by the terms "company culture" and "organizational culture"? That question comes up a lot during my coaching sessions, and we will explore the answer in this chapter. In doing so, you will reflect about your own company culture and identify areas of improvement and ways you can have a stronger voice within that construct. You will also learn a process where you can seek out champions to help you improve your organizational culture.

What Falls under the Umbrella of Company Culture?

In a broad sense, company culture is the way things are done within a company. Culture can be formed by the values of the founders or dictated by the customers, or it can change based on the diversity of its employees. It can also shift due to a merger or acquisition. Companies are currently faced with the exit of baby boomers, the onboarding of younger employees, pandemic fears, ever-changing technology, and a general shift in the market for products and services. All of these variables impact a company's current and future culture. Even teams or divisions within the same company can operate differently. Many of my clients do not think much about company culture until they take a job with another company.

Have you ever left one company for another, only to find some of the following situations?

- No solid career ladder is in place for promotion
- Everyone routinely works past five o'clock and on weekends
- Emails come through in the middle of the night
- Conflict is not resolved, but left to fester
- Managers do not conduct career conversations
- Meetings do not start or end on time, and there are no agendas
- Expectations or job roles are not clear
- There is no formal onboarding for new hires
- Professional development is not encouraged
- There is a lack of psychological safety
- Decisions are dictated rather than made through collaboration
- High employee turnover

If you have noticed any of these situations at your workplace, the company culture may be toxic. The way a company's leaders run their business internally (impacting employees) and externally (impacting customers) is based on their values, behaviors, and habits. Over time, this is simply the way things are done; it becomes the norm. It transforms into the culture of the organization. Company culture includes communication, authority, delegation, level of toxicity, speed of innovation, creativity, hiring philosophy, operating lean, promotion guidelines, and accountability.

Here is the clincher. Culture is neither good nor bad. But culture can be perceived as either good or bad, depending on an individual's own values and expectations. That is why you need to be crystal clear about what is important to you. The less clarity you have about your own values and mission, the greater the chance for a misalignment between you and the company.

Early in my career, I was still heavily influenced by my toxic childhood. I was operating under long-held beliefs and outdated values. I believe I was drawn to toxic work environments because that was my model; it was the only framework I knew. Had I been further along in my personal growth journey, I might have identified the misalignment sooner by comparing the environment to my values and expectations. There are many people who have learned to tolerate and become engrossed in toxic behavior. They do not do anything to change and feel quite comfortable (even thrive) within toxic environments. They might perceive the company's culture as "good" simply because it is what they're familiar with. Assuming you are doing your personal work and striving to improve, how do you know if you are misaligned? And what can you do about it?

What to Do about Misalignment?

For some of my clients, the first recognition of misalignment comes with feelings of frustration, anxiety, or confusion. In coaching, some clients say things like, "Huh, well, this job is different than what I thought it would be." Or, "This is not at all what I was told when I interviewed." Or, "I'm not sure I like this way of doing things, and it will be hard to get used to." Or, "I might have made a mistake by coming here, but I will give it some time."

Pay attention to your feelings, self-talk, and intuition to recognize whether a company or a role is right for you or not. You can also do a reality check with a trusted coach or advisor to talk through what you are experiencing.

If it becomes clear that the company culture is not a fit for you, there are several things you can do:

CHANGE YOURSELF

This depends on what needs changing and to what extent you will be compromising your values. For example, if you are the collaborative type, but individuals or teams in your company are not, then you may choose to work more independently to see how that feels. Some people choose this option as a short-term solution to see how things unfold over time at the company. Sometimes a merger, acquisition, or unexpected change in management will cause a positive shift in company culture.

LEAVE THE ORGANIZATION

If you choose this strategy, be sure you are doing your personal work so that you know what you are looking for in a new job. For example, know your values and strengths to be sure your chosen career trajectory is in alignment with them. If you cannot pinpoint your values and strengths, you may end up in the same workplace situation again.

DO NOTHING

Some people take a wait-and-see approach and tolerate the misalignment. Some of my clients have done this for many years and have become exhausted from it. Again, it depends on to what extent you must compromise your values.

TRY TO INFLUENCE THE ORGANIZATIONAL CULTURE

You may choose to stay with the organization and try your best to help change the culture. This option has some benefits for you professionally. For example, it is possible that you will face misalignment in other companies, so building the skills to influence culture can only help your personal brand. You may also gain a lot of visibility by trying to shift the culture. So it could greatly enhance your career or set you up for a promotion. The downside to trying to influence culture is that it is hard work, can be frustrating, and takes a lot of time, and you may end up still leaving the organization. Either way, it is a very personal decision, based on your values, mission, risk tolerance, and mental energy level. I am going to walk you through some steps that my clients have taken when they have chosen this option. You can try these same steps if you feel there is a misalignment between you and your company:

1. Conduct a gap analysis

    Make a list of things about the company that do not align with your values and mission. Be highly critical and create an extensive list because, after all, you spend approximately ninety thousand hours at work during your lifetime. You deserve to be happy. If you are going to stay and attempt to make a difference, then you need to do an honest assessment and acknowledge the gaps.

2. Prioritize the gaps

    Once you have listed the gaps, or areas of improvement, you need to prioritize them. Let us be honest here: you cannot tackle everything all at once. As with anything, you need to determine where to begin. For some people, they target the easiest gaps first, the "low-hanging fruit." Others focus on the area that is most out of alignment for them—the most important thing, according to their values, that they aren't receiving at work.

3. Champion the cause

    Now you have a cause—something that is important to you based on your values and mission. You can become the champion of this cause! My client Alejandro became the champion of a cause that was close to his heart.

Case Study

Alejandro was a director who had seven senior engineers reporting to him. He was new to the company and realized early on that there was no clear career ladder for his direct reports. This bothered him because his mission was to help elevate engineers to the executive level. In addition to his director role, he championed this cause by working with his boss and Human Resources. He presented a plan that was implemented company-wide to allow this best practice.

1. Build your case with data

    Before Alejandro spoke with his boss and Human Resources, he collected data. He created a proposal based on researching other companies that successfully elevated engineers through a solid career ladder. He also benchmarked departments within his own company and highlighted the number of engineers who had been stagnant in the same role for years. The data helped him to influence and win over the decision-makers.

2. Seek out sponsors

   Even though Alejandro was the champion of his cause, he needed sponsors to help him reach his goal. He started by having a conversation with his boss and then reached out to Human Resources. It is critical that you seek out supporters who offer help or simply give objective feedback about what you are trying to accomplish.

3. Have a voice

   You will find that steps 1 through 4 can be completed independently. But step 5 requires you to involve others. To do this, you must convey your opinion, speak up, and positively influence them. Having a voice is one of the best skills you can build in the workplace, and it will benefit you in many types of professional interactions. It involves being direct, assertive, and empathetic, and using active listening skills.

4. Follow through

   No matter what, you need to either follow through with your cause or hand it off to another competent person. Reliability and consistency are critical when trying to shift organizational culture. You need to earn and maintain the trust of your sponsors and other employees. Remember, your behavior will impact your brand as a leader.

Choosing to stay with a company and influence the culture is risky. But if you succeed, it will pay immense dividends that will be beneficial to your career. In some cases, though, it does not turn out so well. This was the case with Doris, who, like Alejandro, was new to the company.

Case Study

Within just a month of being hired at a consulting company, Doris knew she did not like the culture. After conducting an in-depth gap analysis, she realized that many things there aligned with her values. However, the few items that did not were not acceptable. She took her chances, gathered her data, and tried to find and influence her sponsors. This plan unfortunately backfired because of the toxicity and distrust within the culture. She was perceived as trying to stir up drama and trouble and inflict her "rogue" views on others. Within the first year, Doris left the company and found a more suitable job.

Have you ever had to make a choice about whether to leave a company that was misaligned with your values? If you chose to stay, what steps did you take to become more aligned?

It Takes a Village

Earlier in the chapter, I mentioned that you cannot take on all the gaps at once and that you must prioritize. If you are successful at championing a cause to fill one gap, that process can become your model. You can leverage those sponsors to help you form more alliances and tackle another gap if you choose. At the very least, it will give you good practice at developing your skills of influence and having high-stakes conversations. A healthy company culture is built around the shared values, vision, and mission of its employees, leadership, and customers. That type of environment opens the door for diversity, creativity, innovation, psychological safety, consistent hiring practices, and constructive conflict. While culture change does take a village, it can begin with just one person and build momentum.

Summary

- Culture is based on perception and is neither good nor bad
- Culture is a set of best practices—the "way things are done around here"
- If your values do not align with the company's values, then you most likely will not be happy
- If there is a misalignment you can change as an individual, leave, do nothing, or try to influence the culture
- You can influence culture by championing a cause and forming alliances

ACTION ITEM

Before moving on to the next chapter, please complete the following exercise:

- Using your journal and the framework and questions in this chapter, do an analysis of your company culture in comparison to your values

Chapter 11

IMPLEMENTING COMPANY-WIDE CHANGE

I learned to fear change due to the chaos of my upbringing. In my personal and professional life, I always felt rocked to the core when even a simple event shifted my equilibrium. The slightest instability caused anxiety for me and made it difficult to manage my emotions. In a workplace filled with change, how do you keep yourself grounded, keep your team moving forward during ambiguous times, and be an advocate for change? In addition, how do you manage employees whose negative attitudes can sabotage change initiatives? If you can do these things successfully, you will be known as a change agent. These skills are highly coveted by recruiters and those already in leadership positions. In this chapter, you will gain a better understanding of the dynamics of change and explore how to manage yourself in an ambiguous work environment. Then you will learn how to use those skills to advocate change by modeling the same behavior across your organization and mentoring other change agents.

One of the expectations of leaders is that they adapt to the fast-paced environments in which they work. They need to pivot quickly whenever a change occurs. Yet they must do so in a calm and centered way, while still focusing on corporate goals, team morale, and project execution. That is not an easy feat at all! This is made even more difficult by a natural psychological cycle that each person goes through when they are faced with change.

Workplace Change and the Grief Cycle

In many circumstances, workplace change can be likened to the grief cycle introduced by Dr. Elisabeth Kubler-Ross.[13] Kubler-Ross identified five stages of grief: denial, anger, bargaining, depression, and acceptance. The denial phase usually begins with shock or a refusal to accept reality. Initially, denial is necessary because it protects us from being overwhelmed. It consists of avoidance, confusion, shock, or fear. Anger comes up in the form of frustration and anxiety. Bargaining is a way to try to find meaning by reaching out to others or telling one's story. Depression can manifest as an overwhelming sensation, hostility, or flight. Acceptance is a period of exploration, putting a new plan in place, and moving on. Do you see anything in this description that reminds you of a past or current workplace change initiative? Although people move through these stages at different rates, doing so helps them accept and even thrive during and after workplace ambiguity.

Developing Adaptability to Manage Workplace Change

How can you develop the adaptability you need to manage change at any time, while also guiding your team? It is important to realize that, before you can lead others through change, you must first prepare yourself to do it. Here are some ways you can do that:

---

13 Psycom. 2022. "The Five Stages of Grief." Psycom.net. Psycom. June 7, 2022. https://www.psycom.net/stages-of-grief.

- Proactively stay abreast of industry best practices regarding change management by reading industry magazines, attending conferences, and networking.

- Understand the five stages of the grief cycle and which phase you are in at any given time during a change event.

- Do things outside your comfort zone by taking actions before you are comfortable with them.

- Gather as much information as you can about the impending change, realizing that more information will unfold over time. You can do this by paying attention to company-wide emails, setting up an informational call with Human Resources, or attending voluntary company-wide meetings.

- Analyze the big picture so that you understand why the change is necessary and its benefits to the organization or department. This does not mean you have to agree with it, but you at least need to see it from a strategic point of view.

- Offer to assist with any pieces of the change initiative. The more you help, the more in control you will feel, and the more information you will be privy to as it unfolds.

- Take care of yourself during the change process, and continue to hone your leadership skills.

- Create your own individual change model, so that you have a personalized process to follow when you are faced with ambiguity and need to adapt quickly. This involves steps you take, behaviors you engage in, or people you rally for support.

- Plan for and control the things that you can and accept the things that you cannot.

Factors and Skills to Help You Succeed

Becoming adaptable and learning to manage change takes a deliberate effort on your part. Here are some important factors and skills that will help you succeed, especially during uncertain times:

- Health: good physical fitness, prudent lifestyle, quality time for leisure

- Emotional security: openness regarding emotional and mental health issues, seeking help when needed

- Economic security: additional resources, no debt, stable income, low commitments, reliable financial advice

- Prior transition skills: positive transition experiences, planning, goal-setting

- Supportive work environment

- Transition support: supportive and stable support networks, tolerance, dignity

- Flexibility

- Patience

- Communication

- The ability to reframe events to see the strategic angle

You must master these skills first before you can support your team or become a change agent throughout your organization. You can help your team successfully manage ambiguity by reframing events so that they understand the benefits and long-term impact. For example, many companies go through internal reorganizations once or twice a year. This might seem incredibly daunting, but the following case study shows how beneficial this can be to individuals and teams.

Case Study

Carmella was a client who worked for a company that went through organizational changes every six months. She was frustrated by this because it had been going on for two years and she was always fearful of losing her job. In coaching, we stepped back and took a strategic look at what these changes meant for her. She had never lost her job. She had been transferred to different teams and departments, had new managers, and learned new skills. She suddenly realized that she was being unintentionally cross-trained and now had a cross-functional skill set. She had also gained important skills by working with four managers who all had different leadership styles. This "cross-functional learning" had made Carmella more marketable.

The Importance of Cross-Functional Learning

In the past, it was important to stay on one team in a singular department within the same company for as long as possible to prove your loyalty and become a subject matter expert. Some recent research shows this is no longer the case. The more skills and experience you have in different areas, the more valuable you are to the company. This is just one way that organizational change initiatives benefit individuals, teams, and companies. In addition, successful change initiatives tend to result in higher motivation, expanded skill sets, and decreased attrition. Unsuccessful change management has a negative impact. Here are some examples of both.

SIGNS OF PROPERLY MANAGED CHANGE

- Available forums for employees to discuss concerns and ask questions
- The learning of new skills and the ability to adapt
- Increased transparency and communication
- Increased self-esteem, motivation, and confidence levels of employees
- Reversal of negative and destructive thoughts
- Increased mental and emotional resilience
- Ability to reframe events and remove impediments and resistance to change
- Effectively and effortlessly deal with the pressures of the workplace
- Strategies for transition management that dramatically improve relationships
- Inspired, energized, motivated, and intellectually stimulated coworkers
- Ability to communicate, problem-solve, and resolve conflict in a more effective way
- Develop or improve leadership skills
- Improved job performance and quality of work
- Increased job satisfaction

- Lead by example (even while under pressure) in the workplace, home, and community

- Strategies to become more focused, creative, centered, and decisive

- Overcome the fear, inner conflict, and isolation that accompany transition

SIGNS OF POORLY MANAGED CHANGE

- Increased risk of severe crisis throughout the team
- Extended work absences
- Giving up, gossip, negative attitudes
- High risk of errors or reduced productivity
- Indiscretions or poor strategic decisions
- Dysfunctional communication and work relationships
- Poor team morale and high turnover
- Reduced career prospects
- Rebellious staff, unused insights, dissent, conflict, high-stress environment
- Lack of focus and creativity
- Unhappy clients/customers
- Resistance and fear
- Poor leadership

Based on what you just read, how is change managed within your team at work? Given the benefits of proper change management, it is well worth it to learn to adapt and teach your team the same skills.

It is one thing to support and mentor your team during change, but how do you model that behavior and spread your influence across the organization? How do you formally lead and embrace change by causing disruptions?

Becoming a Change Agent

The term change agent can refer to either an organization or an individual performing at any level within an organization. A change agent is an entity or an individual who has the qualities, skills, and abilities to:

- Be willing to *lead change*
- Have the *know-how* to lead change
- *Reframe* change into potential opportunities
- *Look for change*
- *Be ahead of change*, anticipate change, and appreciate change
- *Make changes work within the organization as well as outside of it*

This seems like a monumental endeavor, one requiring fine-tuned abilities. However, the skills and abilities can be learned and implemented. Being a change agent involves demonstrating outstanding performance in at least the following three major areas of expertise.

1. Balancing Change and Continuity at the Same Time

    - Although continuity is the foundation for an individual and organization to thrive, both must prepare for constant and rapid change.

- One effective method is to create long-term, continuing relationships with internal employees as well as outside partnerships. These relationships or partnerships are invaluable in today's global change environment.

- The sharing of critical information is key for continuity and relationships. With every change comes a crucial question: "Who needs to know about this?"

- Both innovative and continuous improvement ideas must be rewarded and recognized.

2. Knowledge of Effective Methods of Implementing Change

    - The most effective strategy of implementing change is to find someone who wants to champion the new product, service, or idea.

    - Another useful strategy is to find a customer who is willing to work with you to make the new product, service, or idea successful.

    - If this pilot test is effective, it will indicate what, where, and how to implement the new change.

3. Systematic Strategies for Inevitable Change

    - Creating a policy of innovation or of creating change allows for a mindset that views change as an opportunity.

    - The policy should include a plan where you are frequently looking for changes that could be opportunities.

    - Areas to look for possible changes include:

- Inconsistencies in customer behaviors: what they purchase, what online platforms they are using, or the time of day when they purchase.
- Demographic changes: the number of women purchasers, age ranges, or education level.
- Industry or market changes: supply availability, emerging technology, or a new competitor.

- Questions then need to be asked about what kinds of changes might be innovative.

- Related risks need to be identified and then mitigated or limited. This and the prior bullet point can be accomplished with a SWOT analysis (Strengths, Weaknesses, Opportunities, and Threats).

A skilled change leader can guide their team through change, manage multiple change initiatives at any given time, and understand a variety of change models. Below are three common change models that many companies use for change initiatives:

- Lewin's change management model[14]
- The rational approach[15]
- Top-down or bottom-up?[16]

Teams need strong leaders to guide them through chaos and ambiguity. As a leader, it is your responsibility to develop your individual change management skills, and then develop the skills

---

14 Mind Tools. 2023. "Lewin's Change Management Model." Mind Tools. 2023. https://www.mindtools.com/ajm9l1e/lewins-change-management-model.

15 IBS Case Development Centre. 2007. Executive Interviews: Interview with Michael Beer on Change Management. June 2007. http://ibscdc.org/executive-interviews/Q&A_with_Michael_Beer_6.htm.

16 Eveleigh, David. 2019. "Top Down or Bottom Up? A Change Management Perspective." May 13, 2019. https://www.linkedin.com/pulse/top-down-bottom-up-change-management-perspective-david-eveleigh.

necessary to encourage and support change in your organization. But what about people who do not agree, are difficult or negative, and allow their attitude to influence others?

Change Agent Saboteurs

A common name for this type of person is a change agent saboteur. They are stuck in the beginning stages of the grief cycle and, even worse, their negativity can greatly impact change initiatives. Josephine was a change agent saboteur who, fortunately, got unstuck with some outside assistance.

Case Study

Josephine was a sales executive and top performer in a large pharmaceutical company. Her annual sales topped over a million dollars a year. At the beginning of the year, some changes took place in Josephine's company. Her boss, Joan, who was the department VP and Josephine's friend of fifteen years, left the company. Joan was replaced by an interim VP, David, a male who was younger than Josephine. David brought a vastly different culture to the company. Josephine, who liked structure, details, and information, began to panic as changes were implemented. She had several conversations with Joan, asking her to rethink her decision and come back to the company. Although Joan informed her with each discussion that she had no intention of changing her mind, Josephine persisted for months. She spent hours reminiscing over the "good times" when Joan was in charge. She often thought, "This can't be happening to me at this stage in my career." Her peers seemed to be adjusting well to the changes, but Josephine continued to live in the past.

Over time, she developed some mild insomnia and daily headaches. She began to lash out at David by ignoring his instructions, becoming argumentative, and rebelling against his authority. Her sales dropped, and she was no longer performing at her best. She became unsociable and unhappy, and complained often.

After many months of declining health and suffering relationships, Josephine began receiving some outside support. She soon realized that perhaps this change was a blessing, a chance for her to learn flexibility and to look at new possibilities. David had created a few new positions, and Josephine thought she might be interested in one of them. She began to look to the future and imagine the possibilities. She became clearer about her vision and readily accepted outside support and advice from her peers. After a time of doing a bit more inner work on herself, Josephine applied, and was accepted, for one of the new positions.

Consider the following questions:

- How did Josephine's professional challenges overlap with her personal life?

- At which points did Josephine go through each of the stages of grief?

- What would Josephine need to do differently to be successful in her new role?

Mitigating the Risks of Change Agent Saboteurs

As a change agent, it is your responsibility to positively influence saboteurs. And the best way to do so is proactively! This means building relationships, understanding others' perspective on change, providing empathy, and training them to see the benefits of change. Adaptability and flexibility are mindsets, as well as skill sets. Learning and growth can replace fear. If you sense that someone is averse to change, try to get them involved in small changes. For instance, you can allow them to help with the planning of these initiatives and give them feedback. The best thing you can offer during ambiguous times is communication and transparency. Employees fear the unknown, so the more clarity you can provide, the better.

As a leader, you may be privy to information about change initiatives that you cannot share. My clients often feel guilty about this. It is hard for them to support senior leadership with confidentiality, keep valuable information from their team, and share only limited details with that same team. If there are things you cannot divulge, or if you have limited transparency, then be transparent about that. Make your position clear, provide empathy, but enforce the boundaries of confidentiality. Your team will understand, and your actions will also help shift the negativity of saboteurs. Referring people to Human Resources for more information is another great option if you cannot answer all their questions.

You can provide support to people by creating a forum where others can share their concerns, providing frequent updates to direct reports, meeting with your peers to share information, and gauging the level of anxiety of stakeholders. Use your own change management skills to reassure others and promote small wins along the way. If one of your direct reports is a saboteur and your group efforts are failing to influence this person, work with them individually. Help them identify where they are in the cycle of grief and offer support.

HSPs and introverts tend to be more sensitive to change in their environment because they process information so deeply. Be mindful of this as you take steps to support others. Being an HSP, an introvert, and someone with cPTSD, I still have some anxiety when it comes to change. However, through my personal development work and using the tools in this book, I have learned flexibility, agility, and—most importantly—to give myself some grace while under pressure. Change agent behavior involves a strategy that begins with you and is passed on to your team and organization through influence, training, and mentoring.

Summary

- The grief cycle is a natural process that people go through when managing change

- People go through the cycle at different rates, and some get stuck at certain points

- It is critical to learn your own change management skills first before you can influence others

- Change can have very positive outcomes for teams and organizations

- Becoming a change agent means influencing the highest levels of the organization

- Change agent saboteurs can negatively impact change initiatives and organizational morale

- There are many ways to influence saboteurs, but the best way is proactively

- Communication and transparency are critical to reduce people's anxiety and manage change

ACTION ITEM

Before moving on to the next chapter, please complete the following exercise:

- Analyze the three change models and determine the pros and cons of each for your situation

Chapter 12

LEVERAGING YOUR STRENGTHS TO NAVIGATE ROADBLOCKS

Do you want to know the best way to work through roadblocks in your organization? Leverage the very things that come naturally to you—your strengths. In this chapter you will first learn how to analyze your roadblocks. Then you'll discover how to use specific strengths to overcome them.

But what should you do about your weaknesses? Many people spend too much time obsessing about those. The methodology of coaching focuses on leveraging what you are good at and learning to manage what you are not good at. Additional research also posits that ideal behavior is a balance between strengths and perceived weaknesses—being adaptable enough to pull from either, depending on the situation. For example, if you are strong in strategic thinking, you may need to downplay that at times when execution is more important. You will learn ways to become aware of your weaknesses, how to manage some of them through the process of delegation, and what to do about the weaknesses that you cannot delegate.

I highly recommend that you take one of the many free strengths assessments online. Strengths are part of your brand and the value that you bring to an organization. No one can take that away from you! Some examples of strengths are reliability, loyalty, active listening, building trust quickly, staying calm under pressure, motivating others, and being highly organized. Strengths are things you did not have to learn through training and repetition, like skills.

I will venture to say that, at least for me, certain strengths were acquired through repetition. For example, my constant and repeated exposure to trauma taught me resilience and emotional strength. Possibly, if you are reprimanded for being tardy enough times, you will learn to be reliable. Within the context of this chapter, strengths are the positive behaviors that you display when you are on autopilot.

Challenges in the Workplace

In the workplace, many of my clients are faced with daily challenges, microtrauma, and dysfunctional environments. They feel helpless and vulnerable, but they are not using their strengths to overcome these things. As human beings, we tend to focus on the negative. We fixate on our weaknesses and spend countless hours trying to "fix" ourselves. I do agree that everyone can benefit from personal and professional development, and that is exactly the purpose of this book. However, do not focus on, develop, or obsess over your weaknesses at the expense of recognizing and nurturing your strengths. I help my clients leverage their strengths, manage their weaknesses, and pivot back and forth when needed.

Once you know your strengths, you need to analyze the things in your work environment that are challenges to you. That could be a relationship with a stakeholder, a policy you do not agree with, or issues with production or customer satisfaction. This type of analysis takes deep thought and reflection, and it falls under the umbrella of strategic thinking. Many of my clients struggle with this and have received feedback that they do not do enough of it. In part, strategic thinking involves looking at an issue or challenge from a broad perspective and trying to resolve it. My challenge to you is to analyze these types of issues and figure out how some of your strengths can contribute to the solution. Let us look at an example involving my client Vershad.

Case Study

Vershad knew that meetings between the sales team and external clients had a history of conflict. Contracts took too much time to finalize, which delayed production. This created constant fires between departments as they jumped through hoops to satisfy the clients. Even though Vershad was not part of the sales team, this issue impacted his team downstream, and he wanted to help. Vershad knew that two of his superpowers were empathy and the ability to read the room when it came to silent cues and nonverbal communication. He asked to be involved as a mediator at the next sales meeting. He immediately diagnosed multiple issues with the way the meetings were being run, put new processes in place, smoothed ruffled feathers, and had the contract finalized in record time. This is an excellent example of how someone can leverage their strengths once they are aware of them.

The Impact of Trauma and Dysfunction on Strengths

If you have suffered previous trauma or are in a current dysfunctional work environment, it will be harder to discover your strengths. Motivation, self-awareness, confidence, and self-esteem are beaten down by these environments. Your psyche is too busy focusing on survival for you to be a proper advocate for yourself. My strengths were hidden for decades while I struggled to overcome shame, horrific memories, and battered self-esteem.

The dark abyss of violence cloaks a person's shining spirit, gifts, and talents. Even now, I sometimes fail to see an accurate perspective of myself. When I hear feedback about myself from clients, friends, or family, I am sometimes shocked to hear all the positive things they say.

Are you someone who is not aware of your strengths, but others are? In Clarissa's case, others could spot her superpower even before she was aware of it.

Case Study

Clarissa was a client who was a victim of previous personal trauma. While her workplace was not dysfunctional, her trauma kept her from making the impact that she hoped for in her job as an administrative assistant for an event planning company. Her therapist assisted her from a psychological standpoint, and I assisted her with her workplace challenges.

Clarissa's boss, the Vice President of Events, immediately saw her strength of organization. As his administrative assistant, she was efficient, addressed all blind spots, kept him organized, stayed ahead of schedule, prioritized with precision, and was cool in a crisis. She even anticipated his every need.

When the Director of Events went on an emergency leave of absence, Clarissa was tapped to take over organizing the yearly corporate event. Cancellation of the event would impact the whole company. Clarissa was responsible for setting up a location, catering, guest speakers, music, presentations, and an evening gala, as well as coordinating the team that would assist.

It took several coaching sessions for Clarissa to understand that her boss saw strengths in her that she did not. We worked to ensure she had the necessary support from coaching, her boss, her team, and her therapist. As predicted by her boss, the event was a huge success! Even though Clarissa was nervous and unsure of herself at first, the event's success helped her see her own worth at work.

How to Advocate for Yourself

Are you aware of your strengths? Do you know exactly how to leverage them to contribute to your organization, but are too afraid to do so? If this is the case, you are doing your organization a massive disservice! Organizations need people like you, with your unique strengths and brand, to create healthier and more productive workplaces. There are several ways you can coax yourself to let your strengths shine:

- Think of yourself as a servant leader—take the perspective that you are there to serve the organization and to assist with your special gifts.

- Ask yourself the following question: How can I serve?

- Be uncomfortable. Purposely put yourself out of your comfort zone, step forward, and do it anyway.

- Keep a strengths journal. Each day, write down all the ways you are already using your strengths without realizing it. This should make it easier to address a known problem at work that you want to help with or are asked to help with.

At the first company I ever worked for, new hires were not given any formal training on our specialized software. They were left to learn the software on their own, yet were still expected to maintain daily quotas. I learned the software well, like most of the other seasoned employees, and somehow started informally teaching new hires how to use it. I liked training others and continued to do it, informally, as part of my role. One day, the president of the company asked me to give a demo of the system to a group of clients. I was nervous, but did it anyway. Afterward, he told me I had a great knack for training and teaching. That was the first time I realized my strength for developing other people's skills. From that day, my career morphed from technical training to soft skills training, to coaching, to—at times—a combination of coaching and training.

When it comes to your strengths, you must either be aware of them or follow your gut instincts and do what comes naturally to you. Then you must analyze the challenges in the organization, look for gaps, and compare them to your strengths. If there is a fit, then reach out and offer to help. This benefits you in addition to those you'll be helping! You'll get increased visibility, build your brand, and impact the overall organization in a positive way. But what should you do about your weaknesses?

Managing Your Weaknesses

I fully believe that you should always be assessing yourself. It is best to have an active self-reflective practice and be looking for ways to improve. But you must keep this in perspective so that you are not obsessive. There are several ways to assess your weaknesses:

- Start with some self-reflective work. What are the areas that hinder you in the workplace, or areas in which you must improve to keep your job?

- Solicit feedback from others. What are others saying about you? How is your behavior impacting them?

- Think critically about promotions. Are there areas where you need to improve to secure a promotion?
- Seek balance. Are there times when tapping into a weakness might be useful? For example, you may work in an environment that honors your strength of directing others. But that could lead to micromanaging. So, at times, you may need to be less directive and more empowering of others and holding them accountable to manage themselves.

Try to be objective with these assessments, and balance self-improvement with the leveraging of your strengths. When my clients receive feedback from their 360 assessments, it takes quite a concerted effort for me to keep them from only focusing on the critical feedback. We focus first on the positive feedback. Then, once we review the critical comments, we determine which ones are important to work on, which ones are a lower priority, and which ones can be ignored.

My clients are often surprised when I suggest that some critical feedback can be ignored. But it is true. It is always your choice how you want to handle someone else's feedback. Not everything needs to be addressed, and weaknesses do not need to be "fixed," because it is about balance. Plus, you cannot, nor should you, please everyone.

What I do suggest is that, if you receive feedback that seems to be about a weakness, evaluate whether it is critical to your job. If it is, either try to improve it, or delegate it.

How to Manage Your Weaknesses through Delegation

Delegation is a valuable tool, and many leaders do not take the time to develop and use it, do not know how, or do not do it correctly. It can help you manage your weaknesses because you can find others who are strong in that area. But delegation can also be used if you have too much on your plate at work, are constantly putting out fires, or find yourself micromanaging your team.

If you have problems like these, delegation should be part of your daily activities. It is the answer to many problems on the work front. Plus, it empowers your team, so it is a great development strategy. Much has been written about how to delegate, but I have summed it up in six steps.

1. Analyze the skills and strengths of your direct reports. In the same way you should be analyzing your own skills and strengths, you should be helping your team do the same.

2. Assess all projects and tasks that you own. Look at what is on your plate and determine your weak areas and what you can hand off.

3. Compare steps 1 and 2. Thinking carefully about the skills of your team members will determine who will take which tasks off your plate.

4. Develop a handoff strategy and target dates. Once you choose someone to delegate to, you must develop a handoff strategy. This involves clearly communicating expectations, outcomes, milestones, and completion dates. Write down your expectations and answer any questions that come up so that you are both on the same page before getting started.

5. Obtain status updates. In addition to the initial communication of the handoff strategy, it is important to obtain status updates during the delegation lifecycle. Also, make yourself available to give and receive feedback to ensure that things progress as planned. Monitor your own actions to ensure you are not micromanaging. For example, if you are not satisfied with the way things are progressing, do not take the task back. Work with your direct report until they complete the task to your expectation. It may take a little longer than anticipated, but it will be an important growth opportunity for them. It will also be an important lesson for you when learning to delegate.

6. Create a follow-up and feedback loop. Perform one last evaluation of the outcome and give constructive feedback and praise, and document lessons learned.

There may be challenges when delegating, but if you use this strategy, the process will go much more smoothly, and it will empower and motivate your team. By you delegating your weaknesses, your team can learn their strengths, which will allow them to also assist the organization in unique ways.

Weaknesses That You Cannot Delegate

If you determine that there are weaknesses you cannot or should not delegate, and those areas are critical to your job, then you should work to improve them. You would do this by creating a learning plan for yourself. This learning plan is similar to the one you already created in the first pillar. Your learning plan is the tool that helps you stay objective and keep track of all your learning for the year.

A Word about Humility

There are some leaders who are all too vocal and condescending about their strengths and the positive impact that they perceive themselves as having on an organization. Their ego can cause true leaders with impactful strengths to be passive, stay quiet, and lose their voice. As you work to let your strengths shine, I encourage you to practice some of the qualities of a leader, like humility and service. I use these terms in the context of assisting your organization, looking for ways to help, and being genuine and transparent about the strengths and value you bring to the table. My clients, especially those with past trauma, struggle with finding a balance between humility and self-promotion. Self-promotion is not the same as bragging and condescension.

How do you know which one you are doing and how you are being perceived? You need to have a consistent self-reflective practice, using all the tools you have learned thus far, and gather feedback from others on a regular basis. In addition, stay humble by serving!

Your strengths are part of the unique value that you bring to an organization. It is critical that you are aware of them, know how to leverage them, and always manage your weaknesses. Assess the opportunities within your company where your strengths are a good fit to solve a problem or impact an outcome. Then you must teach your team to do the same. Leveraging your strengths is one of many ways you can navigate roadblocks and influence your organization.

Summary

- Leverage your strengths, but be aware of your weaknesses so that you can manage them

- Trauma and dysfunctional organizations can mask a person's strengths

- Keeping a strengths journal is a great way to stay aware of your strengths
- Delegation is one way to manage your weaknesses
- Not all weaknesses need to be improved
- Be discerning about which weaknesses you want to work on, delegate, or ignore
- Humility is important; there is a difference between bragging and self-promotion

ACTION ITEMS

Before moving on to the next chapter, please complete the following exercises:

- In your journal, do a "self-audit" of your strengths and weaknesses
- Practice implementing the six-step delegation process

Chapter 13

COMPREHENDING AND COMMUNICATING YOUR VISION, MISSION, AND GOALS

How do companies of all sizes meet their goals? How do they ensure that everyone is operating in sync and in alignment with the agreed-upon direction of the organization? Most successful organizations have a three-to-five-year strategic plan developed by senior management that gets reviewed yearly. That information is then communicated downward through all layers of management to the front-line people who execute daily tasks. If you are in any type of management role, you will, at some point, be responsible for communicating that strategy to your team.

Many times, breakdowns occur during the communication process. This throws management, teams, and deliverables off course. Moreover, it derails the trajectory of the strategic plan. In this chapter, you will learn how to navigate through these yearly strategic plan discussions, how to translate the high-level information to team-level tasks, and how to effectively communicate it to your team. We will also explore a process called Zooming In and Zooming Out—this helps you develop the ability to shift from strategic thinking to execution.

My clients who have been promoted from lower levels of management to more senior levels are told that they need to shift from being in the weeds with the daily deliverables to thinking in a broad strategic way. They do not always know how to adjust to this mindset. Understandably, they have been conditioned to think about details and tasks, solve problems, be hands-on, and put out daily fires.

However, to be an influential and impactful leader, you need to see the bigger picture of how the company runs, understand what the overall vision is, be involved in strategic planning discussions, and keep your team moving forward. Thinking in the weeds is not a bad thing and, contrary to popular belief, you are not an ineffective leader if that is how you are wired. My challenge to you is to learn how to pivot in and out of the weeds. Learn how to transition back and forth between execution-type thinking and strategic thinking. It all starts with those yearly strategic planning meetings.

Navigating Strategic Planning Meetings

You may not be at the level of management where you're involved in the process of discussing and setting strategy for the year, but that is no excuse to ignore the process! If you are not involved directly in the process, most likely your boss or that person's boss is. So you need to stay in the loop by having consistent conversations with your manager and asking about yearly goals and strategy. Eventually, your manager will give you the most up-to-date information but, even before then, it is critical that you stay engaged. This engagement is necessary for your career and for your team. Plus, staying in the loop with your manager allows you to communicate important needs upward. If you want to have a seat at the table, or at least a voice in the conversation, speak up and stay engaged. My client Ron learned this the hard way, and it severely impacted his team.

Case Study

Ron was a middle manager who was not invited to high-level strategic planning meetings. He knew that his boss was involved in those yearly meetings, so he didn't bother worrying about what went on there. He was so busy that he neglected to read some important emails titled: "Staffing Strategy—Input Needed." He knew his manager made all the staffing decisions anyway, so he allowed those emails to sink to the bottom of his inbox.

He was soon shocked to hear that his team would have a lot more work, even though they couldn't handle the work they already had. He asked why no one was being hired to handle the extra work. His manager reminded him of the staffing strategy emails seeking his input for additional new hires. She assumed that Ron had no staffing needs, since he hadn't responded to several reminder emails by the deadline. By being unengaged, in the weeds, failing to see the big picture, and ignoring a chance to give input, Ron missed a critical chance to staff up his team.

As a leader, you owe it to yourself and your team to take part in strategic conversations. Even if you have nothing to verbally contribute, the knowledge you will gain from being involved is invaluable. You will learn about what is happening throughout the company, customer and product changes, industry best practices, and how leaders collaborate and negotiate with each other. Once the official goals for the year are released, they will typically be communicated to you by your manager. At that point, it is up to you to translate that broad, high-level language into actual tasks for your team. Here, again, is where my clients struggle—in translation.

Translate Strategic Goals to Team-Level Tasks

My clients make the mistake of immediately communicating the strategic goals to their team. Yes, communication is great, but you need to synthesize the information first. Make sense of it in your own mind before presenting it to your team. Otherwise, it will be a jumbled mess. I have seen this happen to my clients, and it happened to me when I was an employee.

On one occasion early in my career, my manager announced in a team meeting that she would be presenting our new yearly goals. She displayed a very colorful PowerPoint slide with four lofty goals and wanted our feedback. The slide read, "Increase Market Share by 10%, Reduce Workers Comp Claims by 25%, Roll Out Updated Processes and Procedures, and Increase Employee Retention by 15%." The entire team glazed over the slides, zoned out, and didn't know how to give feedback, because we had no idea how these goals related to us. What did we know about increasing market share, or increasing retention? We had no idea how these goals related to our daily work because our manager didn't help us make that connection.

My clients often make this very same mistake with their teams, and I work with them to first make sense of the goals in their own mind. Before communicating strategic goals to your team, answer these questions for yourself first:

- How can my team contribute to this goal daily?
- What specific daily tasks can my team contribute to work toward this larger goal?
- How can we measure progress on these tasks?

- How can we track whether the tasks are accomplishing the larger goals?

- Are there any goals that are not applicable to my team?

- If some of these goals do not apply to my team, what assistance can we offer to another team?

- What is the best way to communicate these goals and tasks to my team?

Some managers are so detail-oriented that they cannot think strategically or contribute to visionary ideas. The opposite can also be true, and it shows up when you are trying to translate strategic goals to team-level tasks. If you are one of those people who are wired for strategic thinking and not for details, then you will have trouble with translation. With my clients, we pick apart each goal and discuss what tasks or projects are needed to achieve it. If you are not working with a coach, then I suggest you team up with your peers (they may be having the same problem) or an internal mentor.

Only after fully understanding the goals and breaking them down should you communicate them to the team. That communication process should be conducted thoughtfully and deliberately.

Communicate Strategic Goals to the Team

Even though you want the goals and tasks to make sense to the team, you do not want to make these decisions in a silo or without the collaboration of your team. The act of breaking down the goals and presenting them in terms of tasks is to get the team thinking, engaged, and willing to offer more ideas. Once they understand the information, they most likely will have additional ideas on how the team can achieve the goals. So what you offer them are ideas to get them started with the collaborative process.

This can be done in a team meeting, a special brainstorming meeting with a slide presentation, breakout rooms, or other interactive methods. Have your team answer the same questions you asked yourself when you were originally synthesizing the goals. And you always want to tie in the daily tasks to the larger strategic goals so that the team understands the part they play in the overall vision of the organization. This is critical for morale, retention, motivation, productivity, and engagement. When it comes to overall strategy, employees need to know "what's in it for me." Throughout your meeting, be sure to check for their understanding and pause for questions. After the meeting, request feedback. This method of communicating strategic goals to your team helps tremendously to teach them how to think strategically.

The communication process should not stop with your team. As a leader, you should be consistently managing up to your boss to ensure the team is still on the right track, addressing roadblocks, meeting target dates, and monitoring risks or any need to pivot. I call this process Zooming In and Zooming Out.

Benefits of Zooming Out

Being wired to think in the weeds is a strength, and being wired to think strategically is also a strength. Both are highly coveted leadership behaviors, but there is a time and place to tap into each one. As a leader, it is critical that you learn to pivot back and forth. If you are good at long-term planning, then you might not lead well when it comes time for execution. On the other hand, your strength of execution may not be applicable if you must think ahead and mitigate potential risks.

Decades ago, when running my business as a personal trainer, I failed to Zoom Out. That mistake caused a massive disruption in the execution of my services. My business model was to work with individual clients and also teach group fitness classes. The group fitness classes made up about 70 percent of my revenue, and I routinely taught six classes per day, five days per week, servicing about two hundred clients per month. I conducted these classes within a fitness facility, having an agreed-upon revenue split of sixty-forty between me and the owner. At some point, the owner informed me that she was selling the facility and that the new owner would take over in a few months.

The new owner informed me that she didn't want my classes to be conducted in her facility. I pushed back by saying we were right in the middle of a series of classes and the participants had already paid. Only then did it dawn on me that they had paid me and the previous owner. I was so caught up in the daily marketing, teaching, and registration of new participants that I failed to plan for the sale of the facility. I neglected to Zoom Out, think long-term, and ask more questions about what the sale would mean for my business and clients. As of that day, we were no longer allowed to enter the facility for classes.

After some brainstorming and a lot of stress, I arranged to conduct the classes outside until we could find another location. This was a risk that could have been mitigated had I gotten out of the weeds and Zoomed Out.

Here are some key components involved in Zooming Out:

- Incorporate thinking and planning time into your week—even if you need to block it out to avoid interruptions

- Weigh out pros and cons of ideas and situations
- Anticipate problems and risks, then come up with mitigation plans
- Become curious about what other departments or teams are doing
- Develop relationships across the company so that you are familiar with what is going on elsewhere
- Stop making decisions in a silo—invite others to brainstorm and share opposite views

Here are some key questions to ask yourself when Zooming Out:

- Who else in the company might be having this problem?
- Who else needs to know this information?
- Who can give me an opposite opinion?
- When has something similar happened in the past?
- What is the impact this will have elsewhere in the company?
- Where did we go wrong/right last time we did this?
- What are other companies doing?
- What are the industry best practices?

My client Abby is a shining example of someone who was wired to think in the weeds but, with some help in coaching, was able to create a measurable and executable strategic staffing plan.

Case Study

Abby was a middle manager who was asked to come up with a creative way to staff her team over the next twelve months.

Usually, her manager created the staffing plans, and Abby just participated in the interviewing process. But her manager was going on temporary leave and delegated the task to Abby. Abby did not even know where to start, so she reached out to some of her manager's peers to learn about their process for staffing plans. She also talked with her Human Resources business partner to get their perspective and to understand their larger goals. She then looked at her team's workload, spent some time planning out the projected workload for the upcoming year, and obtained some budget figures from the Finance Department. This all took time, and Abby was diligent about blocking out this time in her calendar weekly. Throughout this process, Abby also reviewed the company's mission and vision.

As she analyzed the data of projected work, she could easily make the case for four new hires. But that did not align with the shrinking budget numbers. We brainstormed in coaching and came up with a proposal for her to request two new hires and two temporary contractors. The contractors could be used during the second half of the year when the workload was at its peak. After that, there was a possibility of moving them to a different team and under a different budget.

Abby's proposal was accepted; it was easy to measure against her data collection and simple to communicate to her team. She was able to align the hiring plan (Zooming Out) with the execution of the work (Zooming In).

Some leaders are already wired to see the big picture and how it aligns with the company mission and vision. Their difficulty, however, is being able to ensure execution. After all, the goal is to get the job done, or the mission and vision will not come to fruition.

Benefits of Zooming In

Earlier in this chapter, I mentioned some key questions to ask yourself before communicating strategic goals to your team. These questions can also be used to train yourself how to Zoom In.

- How can my team contribute to this goal daily?
- What specific daily tasks can my team contribute to work toward this larger goal?
- How can we measure progress on these tasks?
- How can we track that the tasks are accomplishing the larger goals?
- Are there any goals that are not applicable to my team?
- If some of these goals do not apply to my team, what assistance can we offer to another team?
- What is the best way to communicate these goals and tasks to my team?

These questions will keep you and your team aligned with the tasks that contribute to execution. Another important tool to use, whether Zooming In or Zooming Out, is a roadmap. Typically, organizations develop roadmaps as part of their strategic planning process. This tool lists the overall vision and mission but breaks them down into milestones and target dates. When trying to Zoom In, you can look at milestones and measure your team's progress against them or create your own roadmap based on the individual milestones. Donovan was a client who originally had trouble Zooming In but had success when using a roadmap.

Case Study

Donovan was a big-picture thinker, leaving execution up to his team of managers and their direct reports. However, the teams were struggling, not focused, and missing deadlines. Donovan's boss asked him to step in and more closely monitor projects and target dates. This was uncharted territory for Donovan, and he did not know how to direct his teams on such a micro level. In coaching, he shared his company's roadmap for the year. For the time being, we zeroed in on two broad milestones for which Donovan's teams were responsible. We analyzed them, broke them down into small milestones, created measurements, and set target dates. Donovan created a second roadmap that reflected these more focused goals. Using the roadmaps as visuals, Donovan was then able to communicate the yearly goals more succinctly to his teams and track their progress during the year.

Pivoting Back and Forth

There will always be times when, as a leader, you will need to pivot from Zooming In to Zooming Out, or the opposite. It is not about becoming the best at one at the expense of the other. Balance is the key in leadership. Developing this kind of flexibility will help you become more well-rounded, more marketable, and increase your chance of a promotion. You will be able to communicate to your team better to avoid any disconnects and keep them on track with performance. Possessing the skill of Zooming In and Zooming Out will also help you mentor your direct reports so they can develop the same behavior.

One thing you can do right now is find your company's strategic roadmap and pinpoint the area for which you are responsible. Are your team's current daily tasks rolling up to what you see on that roadmap? In what way are you communicating your company's mission and vision to your team?

Summary

- Regardless of your role, it is critical to be aware of your company's strategic plan, mission, and vision
- It is important to be able to pivot from execution to strategy (Zooming In and Zooming Out)
- Have consistent conversations with your manager to stay in the loop about strategy
- You must accurately translate the strategic goals to executable goals for your team
- Blocking time to think and plan will help you to Zoom Out
- Knowing specific daily tasks and timelines is an example of Zooming In
- A roadmap is a tool that can help you either Zoom In or Zoom Out

ACTION ITEM

Before moving on to the next chapter, please complete the following exercise:

- In your journal, create a plan for yourself to Zoom In and also to Zoom Out

Chapter 14

COMMUNICATING EFFECTIVELY TO SOLVE BUSINESS PROBLEMS

During my corporate career, I often faced situations where I received different directives from multiple stakeholders. None of them knew about the other's instructions. It took some advanced communication skills for me to get all parties on the same page. Once this alignment happened, problems were resolved much quicker. Most business problems require some type of interaction with other human beings before they can be resolved. These interactions represent communication, and communication includes verbal and nonverbal behavior. This chapter will help you strengthen your communication skills so that you can relate to others better and resolve business problems more effectively. You will explore how to have an open mind when it comes to solving problems, ways to leverage verbal and nonverbal communication, and techniques that will help you be more collaborative without sacrificing assertiveness.

Problem-Solve with an Opportunity Mindset

In most organizations, problems occur daily, and it is important to address them quickly.

A business problem is generally a question or situation that involves doubt, difficulty, uncertainty, or choices. You can tell when there is a problem because there will be roadblocks, confusion, dissension, angry customers, unhappy employees, and many other business dilemmas. Some common problems in the workplace include customers who return products or conflict between team members. There may also be situations where production is low or employee attrition is high. In an organization, it is everyone's responsibility to recognize and resolve problems at their onset, or they will snowball. Having an opportunity mindset is critical during these times. This means looking at a problem as an opportunity to grow, learn, collaborate, and innovate. Working through a problem with this mindset will take the stress, anxiety, and impulsiveness out of problem-solving.

Without this opportunity mindset, you will have a higher risk of reacting to problems out of fear, anxiety, or haste. Though time is of the essence when working out issues, it is critical that you respond with competence and skill, rather than react with a thoughtless, knee-jerk decision. Thoughtless decisions may, at most, work in the short run but not the long run. Embracing an opportunity mindset changes the dynamic from blaming to owning. An opportunity mindset is the motivation that drives action and gives everyone a common goal.

Think of problem-solving as a fact-finding mission. This is not done in a silo—it involves other people, various levels of expertise, brainstorming, researching, and timelines. The solving of a problem is a project, and a negative mindset shuts down the process. The causes of problems are usually related to three categories:

- Physical causes—Tangible, material failures (like the printer stopped working)

- Organizational causes—A faulty system, process, or policy (like no one knew who was responsible for printer maintenance)

- Human causes—Someone handled a job, task, project, or situation incorrectly or didn't do what was needed (like not providing maintenance for the printer)

Most physical and organizational causes can be traced back to human error. There are many causes for human error, like being new on the job, forgetting, not paying attention, not knowing what to do, moving too fast through a process, or multitasking. Sometimes the employee responsible for the task is the wrong fit, and they make mistakes because they are disinterested. There are also situations where the employee does not have the required skills. Many of these examples can roll up to even bigger problems.

As human beings, we can cause problems and we can solve them, but the ideal diagnosis and result comes from having an opportunity mindset and using communication skills to involve others in the process. What pain points are you dealing with right now that you are solving in a silo? How can you shift to an opportunity mindset? Once you have an opportunity mindset, it is important to understand the behavior that you display when problem-solving with others.

Four Types of Behavior

Verbal and nonverbal cues consist of language, vocal information, and body language. When these combine, they contribute towards what we would describe as our "behavior." These can be considered different behavior "types," and they are listed below with some examples.

Aggressive

Demands agreement of others, irrespective of their rights, thoughts, and feelings. Has concern only for their own wants and needs. "Shut up and listen. Do as I say."

Submissive

Agrees to the wants of others even when it is in direct conflict with their own wants and needs. Feels the need to contradict but is unable or unwilling to do so. "If that's what you want, then I suppose I have no choice."

Compliant/Indifferent

Gives in to the wants/needs of others and is not concerned about doing so. "Whatever you say is fine with me." "I really couldn't care less—it won't make any difference to me what we do."

Assertive

To forcefully promote our ideas to persuade others to follow while recognizing the thoughts and feelings of those people who will be affected by our actions. "I understand your difficulty, but I cannot agree with your solution. We need to discuss the situation and reach a compromise."

Many microtraumas occur in the workplace due to aggressive behavior which forces others to become submissive or compliant. Many of my clients strive to become more assertive. This is either because they decide that they need to become more assertive to be a better leader, or because they have been given feedback that they are too aggressive, submissive, or compliant. In the workplace, assertiveness is typically considered the ideal behavior and the other three behaviors are seen as detrimental to your career. Here are some suggestions for being assertive:

- Decide what you want to achieve and state your position clearly

- Use facts and be objective

- Put thoughts and feelings into words by using positive, strong language

- Recognize that you understand and appreciate the position of others

- Decide what you want and what compromises you are prepared to accept

- Recognize the techniques used by others to try to persuade you to back down: emotion, trivialization, changing the subject, guilt, etc.

- Having recognized these techniques, counteract them by standing firm, remembering your goal, and restating your position as many times as is necessary

- Use assertive language

- Use assertive verbal information

- Use assertive body language

The last three items in the list are examples of verbal and nonverbal communication, which are components of the Interpersonal Communication Model.

Understanding the Interpersonal Communication Model

Interpersonal communication in the workplace is complex, and it is made up of many components. Altering just one of the components can dramatically change your behavior when communicating. Which component can you shift to make your next interaction more productive?

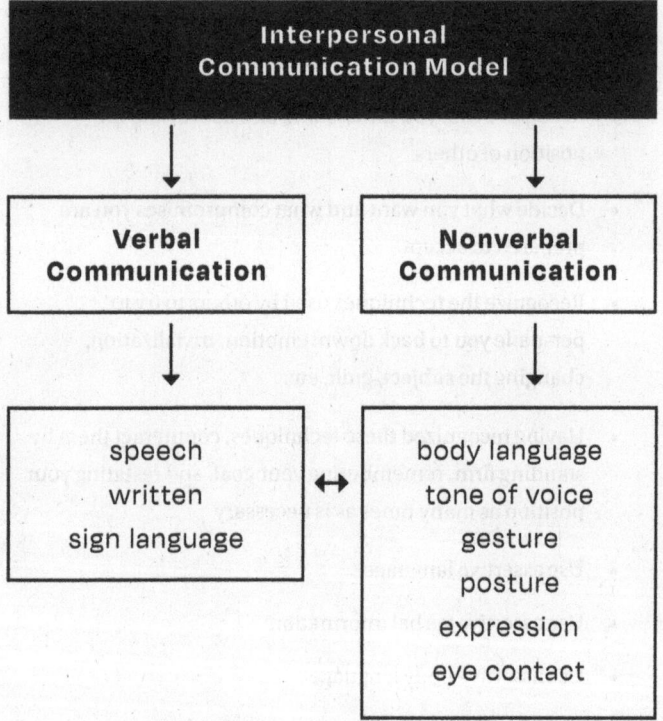

If you are trying to develop assertive communication skills, you can use the Interpersonal Communication Model to do so. Assertive communication allows you to not only build relationships and problem-solve, but to also exude confidence, persuade others, diffuse conflict, motivate your team, and provide feedback. It is a way to productively promote ideas while recognizing the thoughts and feelings of those impacted by the discussion. People who initiate assertive conversations are actively engaged and interested in the discussion. They strongly assert their position, while expressing empathy at the same time.

In an assertive conversation, it is common to hear phrases like, "I understand your difficulty, but I cannot agree with your solution. Let's discuss this further and look at other options." In these types of conversations, everyone is eager to participate, and there is a show of empathy. Assertive communication is different than aggressive communication, where one or more participants may feel harassed, threatened, shamed, or bullied. Assertiveness involves nonthreatening body language and vocal information that opens the door to healthy communication.

Interpersonal communication has many subcategories in addition to those shown in the previous diagram. Let us look at ways to enhance them so that you can have a greater impact when problem-solving at work. Always keep in mind the cultural context in which you are working because interpersonal communication will vary depending on your country or region.

Leveraging Interpersonal Communication Skills

Signs and gestures: Use open hand gestures and extend the hands toward the other person. These small gestures show a willingness to share and understand. Avoid pointing your finger at someone or clenching your fists. Be aware of shrugging your shoulders, as this can show a lack of commitment or interest.

Eye contact: Maintain reasonably steady eye contact, but remember that it is not a staredown. Direct and unbroken eye contact can be perceived as aggressive, but in many instances no eye contact can make you appear weak, submissive, and disengaged. Break eye contact naturally, maybe to view notes or other documents relevant to what you are talking about. Try not to break eye contact to focus on a point behind the person you are talking to, the clock, or your watch. This gives the impression that you are not interested. Others may think that you are not listening and are in a hurry to wrap up the conversation.

Stance/posture: Try to maintain an angle of about forty-five degrees to the person you are talking to, and do not stand directly face-to-face or turn away from them. Do not stand above the other person, especially if they are sitting and you are standing. Try to maintain a distance of at least two feet from the other person. Any closer and you may be invading their personal space, which could seem aggressive. You can experiment with this by standing closer than two feet to someone. Then, watch the other person automatically step back. Keep your hands away from your face and do not flip or touch your hair. These habits can make you look passive, nervous, or flirty. Remain relaxed, but do not slouch.

Facial expression: Movement is the key. Tense facial muscles, like frowning or tight lips, demonstrate aggression. On the other hand, a totally relaxed face shows lack of commitment and suggests boredom. Biting the lip will demonstrate insecurity and, therefore, weakness. Whenever possible, use a variety of facial expressions with movement.

Intonation: Use a variety of tones. This demonstrates interest and enthusiasm. Intonation supports a willingness to understand others while demonstrating a real belief and commitment in your own point of view. Avoid raising the tone on the last word or words of a sentence, as this turns a statement into a question and suggests you are asking for consent rather than making a definite statement. This is sometimes referred to as "uptalk." Try saying the following statement two ways. First, try taking the intonation *down* on the words "two o'clock." Then, try taking the intonation *up* on the words "two o'clock." *"...and I will call you back tomorrow afternoon, at two o'clock."*

Do you see how the first *states* that you will telephone at two o'clock, and the second *asks* if it is okay for you to telephone at two o'clock?

Volume: Shouting can be aggressive, but being too quiet shows weakness and a lack of certainty. Keep the volume strong, but not too loud. Volume can be gauged by listening to a recording of yourself or asking for feedback from others.

Pace: Talking too quickly can demonstrate nervousness or appear dismissive or arrogant, whereas hesitancy or interrupted speech shows a lack of confidence in your own position. Try to keep a controlled pace—not too fast, but moving through what you have to say with confidence and appropriate pauses.

Emphasis: Emphasize words that say what you are going to do, rather than what you are not going to do. When making requests, emphasize what you want the other person to do, instead of what you want them *not* to do. Put an emphasis on words of recognition, words that support your position, and words that clearly state what you want to happen.

Using assertive communication will enhance your relationships, improve your confidence, and help you persuade and motivate others. Which of these skills can you start practicing immediately?

There is one interpersonal communication skill that involves both verbal and nonverbal skills, and that is active listening. Active listening can mean the difference between successful collaboration and a major blowup!

Use Active Listening Skills When Problem-Solving

In addition to the interpersonal communication skills you just read about, there are some very specific verbal components to active listening. They are highlighted in the following model.

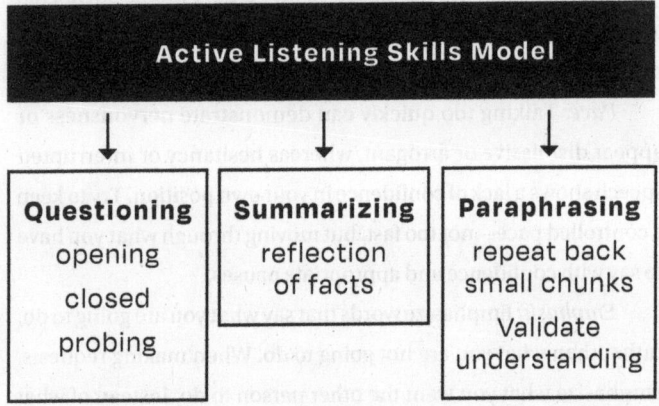

Active listening is much more than sitting silently and absorbing what another person is saying. There needs to be a level of engagement that demonstrates your understanding of the interaction. Some of my clients tell me that they don't need to listen too much because they already know where the conversation is going or they already have a response formulated. This mindset does not help you form relationships, manage conflict, and persuade others. Active listening is the key to doing that. It is important to make each conversation about the other person, not about you or your position. There will be plenty of time for you to insert your thoughts. However, first, you must listen.

Listening also conveys empathy. By asking open-ended questions or summarizing what you have heard, you are demonstrating awareness and concern for the other person's situation. What better way to resolve problems then to let someone express themselves? By entering a situation with a preconceived solution, you are bypassing an important opportunity to connect. Sometimes, just connecting through active listening can bring about a solution when you least expect it.

Now that you are clearer on the components of interpersonal communication skills and their impact, let us explore how to use them in combination with other techniques.

Communication Tips and Techniques

Ideal communication allows for the sharing of ideas in a psychologically safe environment. The Brain Exchange Model, BLUF, NVC, and Beginner's Mind are a few ways you can leverage your communication skills.

BRAIN EXCHANGE MODEL

Brainstorming is a very common way to bring a group together to solve problems. Here is a highly effective brainstorming model called the Brain Exchange. This model enhances team cohesiveness, promotes collaboration, and allows for the healthy expression of ideas with confidence and respect. It can be conducted in a large group or by breaking a large group into several small groups. If possible, use a whiteboard and some sticky notes.

1. Identify the Issue

- Explain the issue

- Sum it up into a one-sentence description and write it down
- Practice active listening while each person is speaking
- Notice your *first* reaction to what they say

2. What Are Possible Causes of the Issue?

- Brainstorm with the group about possible causes
- Determine all possible root causes of the issue and write them down

3. List Possible Solutions

- Brainstorm potential solutions with the group (all responses are good ones)
- Write them down
- Follow your gut reaction, no solution is off-limits

4. Determine the Best Solution (the *What*)

- What solution *feels* right?
- Weigh out pros and cons using *thoughts* and *feelings*
- Don't be afraid to take risks and be creative with the solution

5. Create Implementation Plan (the *How*)

- Write down a detailed plan of action
- Hold specific people accountable for execution
- Set a time frame for implementation

THE BLUF TECHNIQUE

BLUF is an acronym for "Bottom Line Up Front." Many of my clients receive feedback that they are too long-winded when they communicate. In coaching, we practice being more concise by using BLUF. This is a technique where you state your point (or the bottom line) first. Then, you provide two or three short talking points, pause, and invite questions or comments from the other person (or group). You allow the other person(s) to determine if they need more context or not. If they do, then you offer more information. BLUF can be used when writing emails, creating PowerPoint decks, or speaking in meetings. Here is an example of how we altered my client Charlie's narrative before he spoke to his boss, Greg.

Case Study

Charlie was a program manager running a multimillion-dollar project involving five outside vendors, an internal team, and an external client. The internal team had missed multiple deadlines over the course of several months, plus vendors were having supply issues, causing late deliveries. The project was running two months late. The client was furious and escalated the situation to senior management. Charlie explained the situation to senior management and then had to calm down the client. Charlie convinced the client to agree to an adjusted deadline date in exchange for a discount on the final deliverable.

Instead of Charlie immediately communicating the reason for the delay to Greg, he instead used the following BLUF format:

"The client has agreed to an extended deadline date in exchange for a discount on the final deliverable" (this is the Bottom Line stated Up Front).

- "The reason for this is due to internal and external delays that impacted deliverables."

- "The client originally escalated the situation to senior management, but I've consulted with both parties and things are back on track."

- "I'm happy to provide more details if you need them."

Charlie delivered this message verbally, but could have also done so in an email. Using BLUF allowed the same message to be shared in a much more concise way. Greg was given an opportunity to ask questions or request more details. The next time you have a conversation or write an email, try using the BLUF technique.

NONVIOLENT COMMUNICATION

Nonviolent Communication (NVC) is a process of communication created by psychologist Marshall Rosenberg. It is a compilation of ideas about compassionate human behavior and using empathy in conversations. It is based on the concept that needs that are/are not being met cause feelings which elicit behaviors. If a person can determine the needs and feelings of themselves or others, they can determine healthy strategies to satisfy the needs, thereby shifting to healthier behavior. The process of doing this involves providing empathy to oneself or others. Here is an example of how I worked with Cheryl in a coaching session to help diffuse the negative feelings toward her boss.

Case Study

Cheryl was constantly upset with her boss, Jordan, for not acknowledging and providing recognition to her more often. In coaching, we used two key documents that are part of NVC—

the Feelings sheet and the Needs sheet. Cheryl looked at the Feelings sheet and chose two feelings from the list—frustration and anger. These were the two most prevalent feelings she was experiencing toward her boss. She then looked at the Needs sheet and determined from the list that she had a need for validation and competency.

Jordan was not helping Cheryl to get these needs met, causing ill feelings toward Jordan. We then took the next step to determine how *else* Cheryl could get these needs met. After brainstorming, Cheryl realized she could receive acknowledgment and recognition from friends, family, coworkers, and her husband. There were, in fact, many ways to improve her feelings that did not involve Jordan. The final step was for Cheryl to make a request of these other people and ask for periodic recognition, which they gladly agreed to. This allowed Cheryl to get these needs met without having to rely solely on Jordan.

By walking Cheryl through the process of exploring needs, feelings, and alternatives (NVC), I was providing her with empathy by seeking understanding of her situation. With some simple training, you can learn to use NVC in your personal life as well as your professional life. What business problem do you have that can be resolved by using NVC?

You can find out more about NVC and all the available training on The Center for Nonviolent Communication's website.[17] Additionally, a very different but effective way to solve problems is with a Beginner's Mind.

---

[17] "The Center for Nonviolent Communication | Center for Nonviolent Communication." 2019. Cnvc.org. November 8, 2019. https://www.cnvc.org/.

BEGINNER'S MIND

Have you ever tried to approach a problem as if you knew nothing about it? Simply by pretending it was the first time you were ever exposed to it? That is a Beginner's Mind—looking at something as if it were a clean slate. That mindset gives you a new perspective. Here are a few ways to do it:

- Take your business problem to an outside party who knows nothing about it and brainstorm with them
- Ask the customer what they would do
- Ignore current best practices and create new ones
- Ask your children about it
- Gather one person from each department and put them in the same room to discuss it
- Ignore everything you have ever been told about this problem or the solution, and start fresh

Never-Ending Problems

You will always experience business problems in the workplace. Try to shift your mindset to view them as opportunities. That mindset is the first place to start. Then get out of your silo and invite others to interact. Who needs to be part of the interaction to solve the problem? Be mindful that everyone will approach the interaction with a different type of behavior. Everyone will have varying degrees of interpersonal communication skills. Also keep in mind that not everyone is a good listener. You cannot control those things, but you can use every interaction as a chance to practice your own communication skills.

You can use your communication skills in combination with more specific methods and techniques to problem-solve. Brainstorming, for example, helps establish a safe and collaborative environment. BLUF is a great way to practice speaking in a more concise manner. Using NVC shows that you are interested in and concerned about another's needs and feelings. And having a beginner's mind helps you see things with a fresh perspective. Which one of these techniques can you start using today?

Summary

- Problems are an opportunity and can create interaction and connection.

- Four types of communication behavior are aggressive, submissive, compliant, and assertive.

- Leaders should strive for an assertive communication style.

- Interpersonal communication involves verbal and nonverbal skills.

- Active listening is a skill that includes verbal and nonverbal communication.

- Active listening includes the verbal skills of questioning, summarizing, and paraphrasing.

- BLUF stands for Bottom Line Up Front and is a style that states your point in the first sentence.

- Nonviolent Communication (NVC) is a method of communication that involves showing empathy.

ACTION ITEMS

Before moving on to the next chapter, please complete the following exercises:

- Ask for informal feedback about your communication skills
- Implement the Active Listening Skills model to improve your listening skills

Chapter 15

BUILDING STRONG BUSINESS RELATIONSHIPS THROUGH NETWORKING

How much time do you spend deliberately building relationships at work and within your industry? My clients tell me that they have meetings every day. They tell me that they have conversations with coworkers every day. But meetings and conversations are not the same thing as having a deliberate strategy to expand your professional network. You owe it to yourself and your career to weave networking into your daily activities. Networking provides you with the following benefits:

- Visibility throughout your company
- To be seen as an expert in your domain
- A way to communicate your brand
- The ability to promote your team
- An avenue to articulate your desire for a promotion
- An opportunity to express your value through self-promotion
- A chance to learn about others' challenges

- A forum to discuss what you or your team can do for others

- The ability to stay informed on strategic company initiatives

There is really no way to go wrong by incorporating networking into your business activities. However, the mere mention of it in coaching sessions creates a great deal of anxiety for my clients. They suddenly rattle off an entire list of reasons and questions as to why they cannot or do not network. Here is what they say:

- I do not have time for networking.

- I feel guilty for asking other busy people for their time.

- I do not even know with whom to meet.

- What is the difference between internal and external networking? Should I be doing both?

- How do I initiate a networking meeting?

- How long and how often should I be networking?

- What do I say or ask during the meeting?

- Who should do most of the talking—me or the other person?

- How do I do this online? In person?

- Once I start building relationships this way, how do I maintain them?

- What do I do with the information gleaned during networking?

- If I am supposed to be doing this consistently, how do I keep track of everyone I've met with?

- How can I communicate my/my team's brand or accomplishments during these meetings?
- How can I use social media platforms, like LinkedIn, to network?
- I cannot network because I am an introvert.
- Networking is superficial because it is all small talk.
- I do not like to talk about my personal life with business professionals.

These are all very valid and realistic concerns. They were concerns for me as well. As an introvert, it was always difficult for me to initiate contact with strangers. But now, as a business owner, it is critical to the growth and maintenance of my business. When I began to use the following process, I got more comfortable reaching out to others. Now it happens naturally, and I reap many benefits from it. If you want to be successful in your career, then this is a critical activity to do on a regular basis. What causes hesitation for you when you think of business networking? Throughout this chapter, I will address everything on the above list and help put your worries to rest. But first, let's talk about the various types of networking.

Many Ways to Network

Have you ever considered that networking is more than just having a coffee chat with someone? A broad definition of networking is to simply interact with people in a deliberate way. Interaction allows two or more people to get to know each other. And that can be done in so many ways, like speaking at an event, writing a blog, doing volunteer work on your company's behalf, being a spokesperson for your company, or conducting an informational interview. The traditional coffee chat does work wonders to expand your network. But I would like you to broaden your horizon a bit more while reading this chapter.

People get nervous when thinking about networking because they assume they should be trying to "sell" themselves or their ideas. This is not the goal of networking. The goal is to learn about the other person. In the process of doing that, you can weave things into the conversation that allow them to get to know you and your ideas.

Any of the networking possibilities just mentioned can be done internally (within your company) or externally (outside of your company). My client Anthony is a perfect example of someone who used internal blogging to network and showcase his expertise.

Case Study

Anthony was an IT engineer who wanted a promotion. His boss told him he needed to increase his visibility at the company to make a better case for his promotion. A self-described introvert, Anthony did not want to do public speaking at corporate events or meetings. In coaching, we worked on a strategy where he began contributing to the corporate blogs that were posted on the company intranet.

Each month, he wrote about a different topic within his domain of expertise. The blogs were tagged to allow for comments and interaction from readers. After just two blogs, Anthony generated a lot of interest. He began setting up individual networking meetings with those who left comments. In a way that was comfortable for him, he expanded his network and made his brand more visible.

As with Anthony, try to find comfortable venues to advertise your brand and skill sets. If you have a skill for public speaking, you can look for opportunities to present at company events or meetings.

Now let us address some things that might make you hesitant to start networking. You will be surprised at how many of your fears can be easily resolved.

Making Time for Networking

It is true that people are busy in the workplace and time is of the essence. However, I have never heard of a networking request being denied. Business professionals understand the importance of this activity. They are usually very happy to accommodate a request. It may not be immediate, but they usually make time within a few weeks. If you feel guilty about making the request, keep in mind that you have every right to do so. Networking is a business best practice. It is up to the other person whether they want to accept or decline. You must own your part of the communication and they own theirs. So do not let this fear stand in your way.

Identifying Your List of Contacts

For the best networking results, I always recommend that people network both inside and outside of their company. This is how you expand your connections across your entire industry, and even into other industries. For internal networking, you must also expand outside of your specific department and into other areas of the company. The beauty of networking is that once you start meeting people, they usually refer you to others.

To start, make a list of internal people you want to meet with. You should be consistently adding to this list. If you want to do external networking, then access the connections on your social media platforms. As a business professional, you should have a

LinkedIn profile. In LinkedIn, not only do you have your own contacts (people you are connected to), but there is a way to connect with others by searching and filtering. You can reach out to anyone, anywhere, based on geography, company, industry, and other data.

Networking meetings can take place in person, by telephone, or on video camera. The latter two are considered virtual networking. The benefit of virtual networking is that even those who dislike the traditional, in-person method will embrace this process with ease. With this process, you will be able to network across borders from the comfort of your home. Those who prefer in-person networking will now have a secondary option if needed.

So you will have your internal networking list and your list for external outreach through online platforms. But what is the cadence for networking? How do you make time for it?

Frequency and Length of Networking

Typically, networking meetings last about thirty minutes. It is best to schedule them weekly so that you stay in practice with these skills. However, due to busy schedules, some people can only conduct a few meetings a month. Anything is better than nothing. So you will need to use your judgment based on your schedule.

Some of my clients are in full-blown job-searching mode. They use networking to try to find a job—which is an excellent job-search strategy. In these cases, I recommend that they conduct six networking meetings per week. That is three hours of weekly networking. The cadence is up to you and your situation. But it must be consistent so that you can hone your skills. Get into the mindset of weaving networking into work life so that you can build relationships internally and externally.

How to Initiate a Networking Meeting

Once you have determined your list of contacts and the cadence, you want to send your contacts a short email message or a message through LinkedIn. I do mean short—only about two or three well-crafted, spell-checked, concise sentences. Remember, networking is not about selling yourself, it is about developing the relationship. That should take the pressure off completely because you are not trying to sell, you are trying to learn.

Here is an example introductory sentence to send to one of your LinkedIn connections, or to someone on LinkedIn with whom you would like to connect.

"Hello, John. I noticed that we are both in the same line of work and I'd like to connect with you to learn more about what you're doing these days. Would you be open to a brief phone/Zoom chat in the next week or so?" That's it—done. Two simple sentences.

Here is another LinkedIn sample sentence you can use. "Hello, Samantha. I noticed from your profile that we have some professional commonalities. I'm always trying to grow my list of connections and wondered if you have time for a brief networking call later this week."

Here is an example for someone who is already one of your social media contacts. "Hi, Julie. I notice we've been connected for a while and I'm trying to make more time to get to know my contacts. I wondered if you would like to have a brief chat next week."

You can modify these sample sentences in whatever way applies to your style. The point is that they are short, friendly, and an opportunity for you to learn.

If you are reaching out to someone internal to your company, I always recommend that you use the BLUF strategy from the previous chapter. BLUF stands for "Bottom Line Up Front." It is a way to craft a very concise statement through email. Here is an example of how to use BLUF to request a networking meeting.

Subject Line

Request for Coffee Chat (Instead of coffee chat, you can also say informational interview, chat, or networking meeting).

BLUF Statement

Hello, Jan. Do you happen to have time for a thirty-minute chat at some point over the next few weeks?

Body

I work in the IT department and am trying to learn more about the company, including your area and team. Please let me know if I can put a meeting on your calendar so that we can get to know each other.

The terms "chat," "networking meeting," and "informational interview" are sometimes used interchangeably. Use whatever term you are comfortable with. In the past, "informational interview" was used when people wanted to explore other job roles. They would set up these types of meetings to specifically ask about the role. But now the term is used for anyone who wants to learn what goes on within a company, department, or team. They are not necessarily looking for another job.

What to Say during the Networking Meeting

When someone accepts your request for a chat, confirm the day, time, phone number, meeting link, and location if applicable. Then send a formal calendar invitation. This is for you to initiate, not them. If you are having a telephone call, the content should be no different than an in-person networking meeting.

Here is where most people stumble during networking meetings. You are not trying to sell, convince, or persuade! You are just trying to learn! So plan to ask them two to four open-ended questions. This will allow for two-way dialogue without the chance of you monopolizing the conversation. Practice active listening skills. Here are some examples of a few open-ended questions that are perfectly appropriate for networking meetings:

- What is the biggest challenge that your team is facing this year?

- What are some of your objectives for the coming year?

- How have you been able to build such a successful team?

- What can my team do to help resolve some of your pain points?

Create questions that are applicable for the person with whom you are meeting. Listen for commonalities and show an authentic interest in what they are saying. If you can weave your needs into the conversation, then do so, but don't make the entire conversation about what you need. Look for ways you can help them. For example, send them a resource that might help them with their challenge. Refer them to someone in your network. You can also give them a quick tip or piece of knowledge. Be sure to end the meeting on time.

My clients usually worry that they won't have enough questions to fill up the time. The opposite is usually true, and they normally get close to running out of time. You will be surprised at how much constructive conversation can be generated by a few open-ended questions.

A great side benefit that usually happens at this point is that they will also ask how they can help you. You might respond by asking them to make an introduction for you to someone in the industry or to add you to their contact list. This is the start of building the relationship. Always end the meeting by leaving the door open. By that, I mean that you should ask if you can follow up with them in a few months or ask if you can reach out again should you have more questions. Always get permission to connect with them on LinkedIn.

Conducting the networking meeting is a critical step in the networking process. You must prepare for these meetings in advance. Think about who you are meeting with and craft the appropriate questions. Sometimes people send their questions in advance. This gives the other person a chance to also prepare. Use your best judgment. The more you conduct these meetings, the more easily they will flow.

What to Do after the Networking Meeting

There are post-networking activities that should be completed within twenty-four to forty-eight hours after your meeting. If you promised to send them something, send it. If you committed to following up with them, leave yourself a reminder on your calendar. At the very least, send them an email thanking them for their time. You also need to track all your networking activity in a database with notes about the call. This is critical so that you can maintain the relationship going forward.

You can create your own database in an Excel spreadsheet, or you can use a tracking tool called Huntr.com. This tracking tool is meant for tracking job interviews, but it works just as well for tracking networking activity.

Communicating Your Team's Accomplishments While Networking

My clients always wonder how to self-promote during a networking meeting or how to weave their team's accomplishments into the conversation without bragging. This is a skill that gets easier with practice. It happens during the active listening phase, as you are listening to the person's pain points and challenges. This is where you look for opportunities to insert statements about what your team has done in the past relevant to the problem. These are just one or two concise BLUF statements designed to grab their attention. This is why preparation and knowledge of your audience is so important.

My client Shauna precisely inserted her accomplishment statement at the perfect time while she conducted her informational interview.

Case Study

Shauna and Brandi both worked for a manufacturing company. Shauna was in sales and worked with external customers. She was conducting an informational interview with Brandi, who worked in the Product Development department. Shauna asked, "Brandi, what is one of your biggest challenges right now?" Brandi replied that she was struggling to maintain a relationship with an internal customer who was really upset. Shauna seized the moment and said, "I had a similar issue last year with an external customer. I was able to salvage the relationship and save the two-million-dollar contract. If you think it'll help, I'd be happy to share what I did."

Shauna's win sparked Brandi's interest even though they did not know each other well. The conversation shifted to how Shauna used her strengths and skill set to repair a valuable relationship. When Brandi implemented her strategy, she had a similar success.

When networking, you must look for opportune moments to self-promote and highlight your team. Networking, which is often done in one-on-one situations, is also a key chance for introverts to really shine.

Networking and Introverts

My clients who are introverts are often terrified of networking. Additionally, they and others think that networking is superficial small talk. As you have learned so far in this chapter, networking is far from small talk. It is a structured and deliberate approach to building relationships. Introverts are particularly suited for networking due to their advanced skills of listening and processing information. As a matter of fact, anyone who likes to learn is well suited for networking. The key is to shift your mindset to one of helping others. Ask key questions and show a genuine interest in the response.

Introverts tend to have a laser focus. They pay attention to subtle details and have sharp intuition. Because of this, they can get to the root of a situation in a very short time. Sometimes thirty minutes is all they need to establish trust and get off to a great start developing a relationship. If you are a self-described introvert, do not sell yourself short—it is a gift when networking!

Whether you are an introvert or an extrovert, there is an important side benefit to networking that we have not discussed yet. It is the behavior of humility. What does humility have to do with the concept of networking? How exactly does it tie in to building strong business relationships?

Using Networking to Develop Humility

We have established that networking is a way to build strong relationships by learning about another person. I am suggesting that we can take this further and safely say that networking is a way for leaders to develop humility. It takes humility to admit that you do not know something. It takes even more humility to go find the answer by interacting and asking questions.

Many dysfunctional organizations expect their leaders to have all the answers. That expectation causes a great deal of anxiety for some of my clients. Because, as we all (should) know, having all the answers is an unrealistic expectation. While no one can have all the answers, they should know where to go for those answers. Networking can encourage a leader to "learn" instead of "know." It can help the leader build powerful relationships and use their influence for the betterment of the organization.

Summary

- Networking is a way to build strong business relationships

- Networking can be done internally, externally, virtually, or in-person

- Most fears of networking can be overcome with a strategy and practice

- You must prepare for and be consistent with networking meetings

- Networking is about learning, not knowing or selling
- Networking can help a leader develop humility
- Contrary to popular belief, introverts have ideal skills for networking

ACTION ITEM

Please complete the following exercise:

- Choose three people you want to network with and follow the process in this chapter

Conclusion

INTEGRATING AND IMPLEMENTING STRATEGIES FOR LASTING SUCCESS

As you diligently read each chapter in this book, you were introduced to many tools and techniques for personal growth. When coaching my clients, I impress upon them the importance of integrating the concepts they learn in coaching. That is what you will do in this final chapter. You will use the basics from each pillar to start making positive changes immediately!

Chapter 16

TYING IT ALL TOGETHER

Understanding the concepts of this book does no good if you cannot execute them in your daily life. An action plan is critical if you are to integrate all your acquired knowledge. It is even more important if you want to work simultaneously across both pillars. In this chapter you will create an action plan for each pillar. For Pillar One, you will create goals for each dimension of wellness. For Pillar Two, you will choose one organizational change you would like to make and create a plan to implement that change. Let us get started.

Pillar One: Eight Dimensions of Wellness Process

The focus of Pillar One was to develop yourself in each area of wellness. To make good use of that information, you will be creating objectives, measurements of success, and next steps for yourself. You will carry out these processes in the upcoming year.

1. For each of the Eight Dimensions of Wellness, come up with one objective statement that you can commit to for the upcoming year.

2. Be sure your objective statements start with a verb. For example, for the area of physical wellness, your objective may be to "balance physical health." For intellectual wellness, you may want to "increase personal and professional knowledge base."

3. Write these objectives down.

4. For each of the eight objective statements, determine three to five ways you can measure success. For example, balancing your physical health may involve getting your blood pressure to a certain measurement, getting one extra hour of sleep each night, and exercising four days per week.

5. Write these down next to each objective statement. These are considered your key results. Because they are clearly measurable, you will feel accomplished once you execute them.

6. Then, decide on five to six steps you need to take to achieve those key results. To achieve the three results related to physical wellness, you may need to work with a dietitian to alter your diet, check your blood pressure daily, go to bed earlier each night, join a gym, and work with a personal trainer.

7. Write these down also. This takes a bit of thought, but, when you are finished, you will have a twelve-month plan to move forward in eight areas of your life.

Your result from this exercise should be goals for one year and a plan to execute them. This should be updated in the fourth quarter of each year for the upcoming year.

Pillar Two: Organizational Impact Process

To integrate the information you learned in Pillar Two, you will need to think of one organizational challenge that you are having. Think of something you would like to change so that you can have an impact on your organization. The instructions below will guide you through a plan to initiate that change and how to measure its success. The most common organizational changes my clients seek out are development of diversity programs, implementing more effective employee onboarding, and creating more efficient systems of communication.

1. Write down the organizational challenge that you would like to change.

2. List a one-sentence brand statement or mission statement for yourself. This will be your North Star as you undertake this initiative.

3. In your own words, define your company culture.

4. List the people who will support you with this initiative.

5. List the people you need to influence and the strengths you can leverage to do so.

6. Evaluate how this initiative aligns with the company's vision, mission, and goals.

7. Develop a BLUF statement or PowerPoint deck so that you can present your idea to those you want to influence.

8. Determine one key relationship you would like to build because of this change.

9. Identify how you will measure your success with this initiative. What will be the final result?

10. What is your next step toward this initiative?

If you have made it this far, you will now have a plan to initiate one organizational change. Your plan will be based on the content from Pillar Two. If you are struggling to answer number ten in the list, I recommend that you work with a coach or a mentor to help you move forward.

CONCLUDING THOUGHTS

Writing this book started as a thought buried deep in the back of my mind decades ago. At that time, I began to write my autobiography. But something did not feel right, so I stopped. I now know that I needed to progress further on my journey; I needed to have more experiences and go through more healing. Then I needed to learn how to process all of that and apply the practical tools and strategies I discovered along the way. Having experiences is meaningless unless you can "make meaning" out of them. That is what I have been doing for decades, and I have no doubt that will continue.

Though my autobiography was put on hold, I reveled in realizing how much my clients were growing and benefiting from my coaching. I knew I was doing something unique when I saw their successes and received their feedback. My experiences helped form my perspective, insights, style, personality, and method of coaching. That combination created a skill set that helps people transform. Because of what I have been through, I consider myself fearless—and I help my clients become fearless too.

My clients' worlds shift, personally and professionally, with their hard work and my techniques. It took me some time to realize the magnitude of that. But, once I did, I knew it was time to write a book to acknowledge their successes and provide my methods to you. This book is the vehicle that is helping me to get the message out to all of you. I am passionately committed to helping others who have never even met me. I want to give everyone the framework and techniques to make sense of their own experiences. Whether you are a leader, an aspiring leader, or an individual contributor in the workplace, you can leverage your experiences to be even better.

My intent is for you to use this book as your guide and refer to it often while on your journey. I am thrilled to tell you that a second book, a workbook, and an online course are all on the way! The second book will address a third pillar: how to use these techniques to transform your team. Your responsibility as a leader begins by first transforming yourself, then your organization, and finally—your team! I invite you to contact me with your feedback, insights, and comments, and to tell me how your journey is going. You can do that at monique@mdconsultingglobal.com. Also, please visit my website at www.mdconsultingglobal.com for more valuable information, to subscribe to my blog, listen to my talk radio show called *Leading with Intention*, and connect with me on social media. I wish you the best!

BIBLIOGRAPHY

"7 Behaviors That Put Entrepreneurs at Risk | SCORE." n.d. Www.score.org. https://www.score.org/event/7-behaviors-put-entrepreneurs-risk.

American Psychiatric Association. 2022. "What Is Posttraumatic Stress Disorder (PTSD)?" Psychiatry.org. American Psychiatric Association. November 2022. https://www.psychiatry.org/patients-families/ptsd/what-is-ptsd.

Bankrate.com. n.d. "More than 1 in 3 Americans Would Go Into Debt to Pay a $1,000 Emergency Expense." https://www.bankrate.com/pdfs/pr/20190116-january-fsi.pdf.

"The Center for Nonviolent Communication | Center for Nonviolent Communication." 2019. Cnvc.org. November 8, 2019. https://www.cnvc.org/.

Esty, Daniel C, and Andrew Spencer Winston. 2009. *Green to Gold: How Smart Companies Use Environmental Strategy to Innovate, Create Value, and Build a Competitive Advantage*. Hoboken, N.J.: Wiley.

Eveleigh, David. 2019. "Top Down or Bottom Up? A Change Management Perspective." May 13, 2019. https://www.linkedin.com/pulse/top-down-bottom-up-change-management-perspective-david-eveleigh/.

Gillihan, Seth J. 2016. "21 Common Reactions to Trauma." Psychology Today. September 7, 2016. https://www.psychologytoday.com/us/blog/think-act-be/201609/21-common-reactions-trauma.

IBS Case Development Centre. 2007. Executive Interviews: Interview with Michael Beer on Change Management. June 2007. http://ibscdc.org/executive-interviews/Q&A_with_Michael_Beer_6.htm

Johnson, Craig. 2021. "9 Ways to Donate Old Cell Phones." Clark Howard. February 5, 2021. https://clark.com/cell-phones/donate-old-cell-phones/.

Mind Tools. 2023. "Lewin's Change Management Model." Mind Tools. 2023. https://www.mindtools.com/ajm9l1e/lewins-change-management-model.

"National Prescription Drug Take Back Day." n.d. Www.deadiversion.usdoj.gov. https://www.deadiversion.usdoj.gov/drug_disposal/takeback/.

"New_home." n.d. Tension, Stress and Trauma Release: TRE®. https://traumaprevention.com/.

Psycom. 2022. "The Five Stages of Grief." Psycom.net. Psycom. June 7, 2022. https://www.psycom.net/stages-of-grief.

"Quiz | Emotional Agility." n.d. Susan David, PhD. https://www.susandavid.com/quiz.

Sharma, Robin S. 2010. *The Leader Who Had No Title: An Inspiring Story about Working (and Living) at Your Absolute Best.* London: Simon & Schuster.

Sherin, Jonathan E, and Charles B Nemeroff. 2011. "Post-Traumatic Stress Disorder: The Neurobiological Impact of Psychological Trauma." *Dialogues in Clinical Neuroscience* 13 (3): 263–78. https://www.ncbi.nlm.nih.gov/pmc/articles/PMC3182008/.

"When Domestic Violence Comes to Work." n.d. Www.shrm.org. https://www.shrm.org/topics-tools/news/risk-management/domestic-violence-comes-to-work.

REFERENCES

"5-Steps-Setting-Goals-PDF _1_-3_3_.Pdf." n.d. Google Docs. https://drive.google.com/file/d/11Ztgo_OuXkziYgruMZN4cbGOVE9G1Sk6/view.

Aguilar, Elena. 2013. "A Coaching Framework for Thinking before Acting." *Education Week*, October 21, 2013, sec. Education. https://www.edweek.org/education/opinion-a-coaching-framework-for-thinking-before-acting/2013/10.

BetterHelp. 2018. "What Is C-PTSD? (Complex Post-Traumatic Stress Disorder)." *YouTube*. https://www.youtube.com/watch?v=NeQ8bgUAnFg.

Bowman, Nina A. 2019. "How to Demonstrate Your Strategic Thinking Skills." Harvard Business Review. September 23, 2019. https://hbr.org/2019/09/how-to-demonstrate-your-strategic-thinking-skills?utm_medium=email&utm_source=newsletter_weekly&utm_campaign=weeklyhotlist_not_activesubs&referral=00202&deliveryName=DM50907.

Chamberlin, Jamie. 2014. "Retiring Minds Want to Know." *Https://www.apa.org*, January 2014. https://www.apa.org/monitor/2014/01/retiring-minds.

Church, Allan, and Jay Conger. 2018. "When You Start a New Job, Pay Attention to These 5 Aspects of Company Culture." Harvard Business Review. June 28, 2018. https://hbr.org/2018/03/when-you-start-a-new-job-pay-attention-to-these-5-aspects-of-company-culture.

Conti, Paul. 2021. *Trauma: The Invisible Epidemic: How Trauma Works and How We Can Heal from It*. Boulder, Colorado: Sounds True.

"Developing Intellectual Wellness | Michael Ebinger | TEDxSpokane." n.d. Www.youtube.com. https://www.youtube.com/watch?v=K5ulPdEejjw.

"Do You Have a Fixed or Growth Mindset? | Walden University." n.d. Www.waldenu.edu. https://www.waldenu.edu/online-masters-programs/ms-in-psychology/resource/do-you-have-a-fixed-or-growth-mindset?utm_source=LinkedIn&utm_medium=PSC&utm_campaign=SEO&utm_content=MS%20Psych#__prclt=4OETmD7Q.

Gallo, Amy. 2017. "What to Do When You're Feeling Distracted at Work." Harvard Business Review. December 20, 2017. https://hbr.org/2017/12/what-to-do-when-youre-feeling-distracted-at-work.

Green, Alison. 2020. "My Colleague Keeps Hijacking Our Meetings: How do I shut him down?" Inc.com. Sep 8, 2020. https://www.inc.com/alison-green/my-colleague-keeps-hijacking-our-meetings.html.

"How to Master the Art of Bragging like a Pro." n.d. Www.linkedin.com. https://www.linkedin.com/pulse/how-master-art-bragging-like-pro-amy-elisa-jackson/.

Ioannou, Charlie. 2012. *SWOT Analysis—An easy to understand guide*. Kindle.

Kiyosaki, Robert. 2017. *Rich Dad Poor Dad: 20th Anniversary Edition: What the Rich Teach Their Kids About Money That the Poor and Middle Class Do Not!* Brilliance Audio.

Maxwell, John C. 2015. *Mentoring 101: What Every Leader Needs to Know.* Nashville, TN: HarperCollins Leadership (Audio).

Mckee, Annie. 2015. "How to Help Someone Develop Emotional Intelligence." Harvard Business Review. April 24, 2015. https://hbr.org/2015/04/how-to-help-someone-develop-emotional-intelligence.

"MindTools | Home." n.d. The Situation-Behavior-Impact™ Feedback Tool. Www.mindtools.com. https://www.mindtools.com/ay86376/the-situation-behavior-impact-feedback-tool.

Orman, Suze. 2000. *The Courage to Be Rich: The Financial and Emotional Pathways to Material and Spiritual Abundance.* Manhattan, N.Y.: Random House Audio.

Scott, Gini Graham. 2019. *10 Ways to Analyze Your Own Strengths, Weaknesses, Opportunities, and Threats.* San Ramon, CA: Changemakers Publishing.

"Seven_faces_of_learning_agility.pdf." n.d. Google Docs. https://drive.google.com/file/d/1fv8dJOA6gcpFCfCeVCu3nf5CYL7uVKq7/view.

Simpson, Douglas. *Coloring Stress and Depression Away with Adult Coloring Books: How to Color Adult Coloring Books Like a Maestro to Overcome Depression, Anxiety, and Stress (Habit of Success) (Volume 11).* 2020. Dragon God Inc.

Sinek, Simon. 2009. "How Great Leaders Inspire Action." Ted.com. TED Talks. September 2009. https://www.ted.com/talks/simon_sinek_how_great_leaders_inspire_action.

Stanier, Michael Bungay. 2016. *The Coaching Habit: Say Less, Ask More & Change the Way You Lead Forever*. Toronto, On, Canada: Box Of Crayons Press.

TEDx Talks. 2018. "Breaking the Silence about Childhood Trauma | Dani Bostick | TEDxGreenville." *YouTube*. https://www.youtube.com/watch?v=8NkZO3_h7vI.

TEDx Talks. 2019. "Trauma Not Transformed Is Trauma Transferred | Tabitha Mpamira-Kaguri | TEDxOakland." YouTube Video. *YouTube*. https://www.youtube.com/watch?v=b4loBphYCXI.

Walker, Pete. 2021. *Complex PTSD: From Surviving to Thriving*. St. Peters, MO: Tantor and Blackstone Publishing (Audio).

"Wheel of Consent." n.d. Art of Consent. https://www.artofconsent.co.uk/wheel-of-consent.

"Why Wellness Is the Secret to Personal and Professional Success | Reena Vokoun | TEDxDelthorneWomen." n.d. Www.youtube.com. https://www.youtube.com/watch?v=9_e5sjGLbhQ.

Yohn, Denise Lee. 2021. "Company Culture Is Everyone's Responsibility." Harvard Business Review. February 8, 2021. https://hbr.org/2021/02/company-culture-is-everyones-responsibility.

INDEX

Introduction

anxiety	11–14
boss, bosses	11, 13
Complex Post-traumatic Stress Disorder (cPTSD)	10
depression	13
dysfunction	10, 13–15
Eight Dimensions of Wellness	20
gaslighting	11
Highly Sensitive Person (HSP)	14–15
leader	10–11, 13–16
microtrauma	10–13, 15–16
pillar	17
psychological safety	11–12
PTSD	12
trauma-sensitive leaders	14

Ch. 1

body composition	25–27
cardiorespiratory endurance	25
eating habits	23, 26, 29–33, 38
embodiment practice	22, 40
environmental toxins	33–34
exercise	21–29, 32, 35–40
fitness	24–29, 35
flexibility	21, 25–26
insomnia	22, 35–36
intuitive eating	29–30

journal	23, 35, 41
muscular endurance and strength	25-26
nutrition	21, 23, 27, 29-32, 34, 39-40, 42
self-care	21, 25, 33, 39-40
stress	21-23, 25-28, 31, 33, 35-37, 39-42
peak performance	21
physical wellness	21-25, 28, 31, 33, 39-42
travel exercise plan	36-38

Ch. 2

feedback	50-51
intellectual wellness	44, 46-47, 49, 52-53
knowledge gaps	45, 49-51
learning plan	52
personal knowledge	47-48
professional knowledge	47-48, 53
resource library	52-53

Ch. 3

breathwork	60-61
emotional agility	57
emotional wellness	54-57, 59-60, 62-63
Impostor Syndrome	59, 61
journal	58-60, 64
meditation	60-61
sound	61
yoga	62

Ch. 4

boundaries	65, 67–69, 71
expectations	67–71, 73–74, 76–77
managing conflict	67, 71, 74
relationships	65–68, 71–73, 75–77
relationship wellness	65, 67, 71–72, 76
shared values	67, 71–72

Ch. 5

ancient belief systems	79, 83
inner peace	79, 85
inner voice	80, 84–85
interconnectedness	82
intuition	78–79, 81–83
religion	78–79, 82–83
spirituality	78–91

Ch. 6

corporate social responsibility (CSR)	96–97, 102–103
Environmental Management System (EMS)	97–98, 103
environmental stewardship	92, 95–96, 98
environmental wellness	92–93, 96, 98, 101–103
personal safety	92, 98, 100–101, 103
psychological safety	100–101, 103
volunteering	94, 99, 102–103

Ch. 7

career passion	105–106
individual development plan	104, 112
influence	109–110

interview tips 112–113
mentor 110, 115
promotions 104–105, 107, 110–112, 114–115
strengths 107–110, 115
undeveloped skill set 105, 107

Ch. 8

budgeting 116–118, 126
debt 119–120, 126
financial planning 116, 118–122, 126
retirement planning 116, 121
financial wellness 116, 120–121, 124–126

Ch. 9

behaviors 137, 139–141
personal branding 139–141
mission 137–141
values 133–140
vision 137–141

Ch. 10

company culture 142–143, 145, 149–150
company misalignment 144–146
gap analysis 147, 149
sponsors 148–149

Ch. 11

change agent 151, 154, 158, 164
change agent saboteur 161–162

cross-functional learning	155
grief cycle	152–153, 161, 164
workplace change	152

Ch. 12

advocate	168, 170
delegation	166, 173–174, 176
humility	175–176
roadblocks	166, 175
weaknesses	166–167, 171–176
workplace challenges	169

Ch. 13

strategic planning	177–179, 186, 188
translating goals	180–181
Zooming In	177, 185–188
Zooming Out	177, 182–188

Ch. 14

active listening skills	198–200, 205–206
assertiveness	189, 192–195, 205
Beginner's Mind	199, 204–205
behavior for problem-solving	189–191, 194–195, 198
Bottom Line Up Front (BLUF)	199, 201–202, 205
Brain Exchange Model	199
communication skills	189, 191, 194–199, 204–206
emphasis	197
eye contact	194–196
facial expression	196

Interpersonal Communication Model   193–195, 197–199, 204–205
intonation   196
Nonviolent Communication (NVC)   199, 202–203, 205
opportunity mindset   189–191
pace   197
problem-solving   189–191, 194–195, 198
signs and gestures   195
stance and posture   196
volume   197

Ch. 15

blogging   209–210
contacts and connections   211–213, 216
introverts   209–210, 218, 220
LinkedIn   209, 212–213, 216
humility   218–220
networking   207–220
post-networking activities   216

ABOUT THE AUTHOR

As an in-demand executive coach, dynamic speaker, successful author, and focused and motivating trainer devoted to her craft, Monique Daigneault provides a highly coveted service to corporate leaders worldwide using internationally accepted standards as well as her personally honed methodology.

After dropping out of high school, Monique eventually began pursuing higher education, all while working as a single parent with two young children and experiencing financial challenges, as well as physical and mental health issues. She struggled with panic attacks and complex post-traumatic stress disorder from years of growing up in an abyss of violence and shame. However, she developed a unique skill of harnessing the transformative power of trauma by leveraging her painful past and structuring her coaching approach around a process that allows her to draw from her personal experiences to advocate for others. With an indomitable spirit, a results-driven work ethic, and an enthusiastic commitment to performance improvement, she partners with clients from all over the world, providing practical tools to help catalyze change and facilitate evolution in their personal and professional lives.

As president, CEO, and executive coach at MD Consulting, Monique is also the insightful radio show host of *Leading with*

Intention, a weekly program that broadcasts live in twenty countries and features extraordinary leaders and coaches from around the world. She helps empower leaders to shift corporate culture, build business agility, resilience, and influence, and facilitate transformation in the lives and organizations they lead.

Monique received an MS in Industrial and Organizational Psychology from Capella University. Furthermore, she earned two business degrees and seven additional certifications from other accredited institutions. She is an ICF-trained, internationally recognized coach and IAPC&M accredited executive coach, and received the BetterUp Fellow Coach designation. Since 2019, she has volunteered at VaughanTown, teaching business English as a Second Language to European nationals in a weeklong English immersion program in Spain. Additionally, she volunteers 20 percent of her time to pro bono coaching projects, teaching English abroad, and helping foreign business executives improve business skills through organizations including Amnesty International USA and the Humanitarian Coaching Network.

Monique realizes that, while she cannot change her past, she will not be reduced by it. She views her healing as a continuous journey that she uses in her work to help shape a robust workplace culture and healthy individuals.

Mango Publishing, established in 2014, publishes an eclectic list of books by diverse authors—both new and established voices—on topics ranging from business, personal growth, women's empowerment, LGBTQ studies, health, and spirituality to history, popular culture, time management, decluttering, lifestyle, mental wellness, aging, and sustainable living. We were named 2019 *and* 2020's #1 fastest growing independent publisher by *Publishers Weekly*. Our success is driven by our main goal, which is to publish high-quality books that will entertain readers as well as make a positive difference in their lives.

Our readers are our most important resource; we value your input, suggestions, and ideas. We'd love to hear from you—after all, we are publishing books for you!

Please stay in touch with us and follow us at:

Facebook: Mango Publishing
Twitter: @MangoPublishing
Instagram: @MangoPublishing
LinkedIn: Mango Publishing
Pinterest: Mango Publishing
Newsletter: mangopublishinggroup.com/newsletter

Join us on Mango's journey to reinvent publishing, one book at a time.

www.ingramcontent.com/pod-product-compliance
Ingram Content Group UK Ltd.
Pitfield, Milton Keynes, MK11 3LW, UK
UKHW021108140225
455015UK00036B/392